God Always Says Yes

BY THE SAME AUTHOR

A Letter to Adam
Seed of the New Age
Light Up Your Haunted House

God Always Says Yes

Sue Sikking

DeVORSS & COMPANY
P.O. BOX 550
MARINA DEL REY, CA 90294

Copyright © 1968 by Sue Sikking
All Rights Reserved

ISBN: 0-87516-545-1
Library of Congress Catalog Card Number 68-18079

Printed in the United States of America

PREFACE—THE REASON

This is our world, yours and mine, and we have brought it forth with our minds, which are the womb of the outer world. Man was created with the ability to receive ideas, dwell upon them, and carry them forth into expression. If we would change our world we must change our minds. This is not a new teaching, for long ago a great teacher reminded us, "Be ye transformed, by the renewing of your mind" (Rom. 12:2). The way to newness of life is the same today as then.

There is a great affirmative Power within every human form. There is an All-Knowing Presence within us that always says "Yes!" It is that something that has kept every man on the path toward some goal since the beginning of time. It is the power that fulfills our destiny, the spur to all progress.

Scripture tells us (in II Cor. 1:17–20) that with a worldly man there is always Yes and No, but with God it is always Yes. The things existing in your life here and now were brought forth by your own believing—there is no other way. Believing is a great invisible movement through the mind of the individual. We are not always consciously aware of our believing, but without it we cannot explain our lives. The law of life responds to believing in its entirety. Whether we believe the highest possible ideals or the most dreaded and fearful thought, all power is brought into play by this inherent action within us. God always says Yes to the power of choice in our minds.

It is not your family or background, your education, opportunities, or the material wealth you have or do not have that will determine your destiny. It is what you believe to be true or false or in between. We are not fully aware of our involvement in the world we call ours. *All* is ours that we focus upon, intentionally or unintentionally, for all the power of the universe moves to make it so.

The law of life fulfills our desires, or it fulfills our worries and our fears. With God there is no distinction. The answer is always Yes. The choice is ours.

If you believe and say, "I am lonely, unhappy, poor" or "I am rich, vital, and fulfilled," all power rushes to support your belief. All your fears are answered, but the longings of your heart are also answered. As you think, speak, and act, there is always this response. As you understand this mighty power and your use of it, you have the answer to your own life.

We are told to repent—and to repent, according to Webster, simply means to change one's mind. Take time to examine your own mind and find the secret of life. Life is the realm of accepted thoughts, whether they are true or untrue. Each of us is the creator of his own environment, and unless we choose it there can be no change, for God always says Yes!

Sue Sikking

CONTENTS

1. Crumbling Walls   11
   WHO ARE WE? . . . THE CROSSROAD OF UNDERSTANDING . . . LOST IN DIFFERENCES

2. The New Way of Life   21
   THE FORGOTTEN SOURCE . . . WHAT MUST WE THINK? . . . LOST IN SYMBOLS . . . TRUE EQUILIBRIUM

3. The Unfinished Story   31
   LIFE IS A PROCESS . . . MAN IS THE FINISHER . . . OUR TRUE VOCATION

4. The Law of God Is Completion   42
   THE LAW OF RELATIVITY . . . THE LAW OF VIBRATION . . . THE LAW OF POLARITY . . . THE LAW OF RHYTHM . . . THE LAW OF GENDER

5. The Untouchable You   57
   EQUALIZE THE PRESSURES . . . LET GO OF THE PAST . . . IN THE IMAGE OF GOD . . . FORGETFULNESS OF GOD . . .

THE UNTOUCHABLE PART OF YOURSELF . . . THE VALUE OF NOT THINKING . . . THE TWO THINGS MAN MUST DO

6. Am I My Brother's Keeper?   70
   WHEN THE ANSWER IS NO . . . WHEN THE ANSWER IS YES . . . FIND YOUR OWN WAY . . . WE NEED EACH OTHER . . . MAKE NO SMALL PLANS . . . THE TRANSPARENT RACE

7. Choice Is Our Privilege   80
   FREEDOM UNDER GOD . . . SAFETY IN UNION . . . OUR DIVINE PLACE IN THE UNIVERSE . . . TO HOLD IS TO LOSE . . . ACTING ON FAITH . . . WHAT IS "PROPER"? . . . DON'T ASK WHY

8. The Meaning of Prayer   94
   PRAYER IS ACCEPTANCE . . . PRAYER IS PRAISE . . . THE WRONG PRAYER . . . YOU ARE IMPORTANT TO GOD . . . PRAYER LETS YOU KNOW . . . WHY DO YOU PRAY? . . . WHAT DOES PRAYER BECOME? . . . NOW IS THE TIME TO PRAY . . . HOW TO PRAY . . . WHY SAY "AMEN"?

9. Meet Yourself   108
   LIFE IS TO BE MET . . . THE GREAT CONTRADICTION . . . DO NOT INTERFERE WITH YOUR OWN GOOD

10. The Death of Death   116
    WHAT MUST WE DO? . . . MAN MUST CHANGE . . . BELIEVING IS THE SECRET

11. Life Is the Activity of God   129
    HOW DO WE DO IT?

12. The Beginning, Not the End   137
    LOOK FORWARD

God Always Says Yes

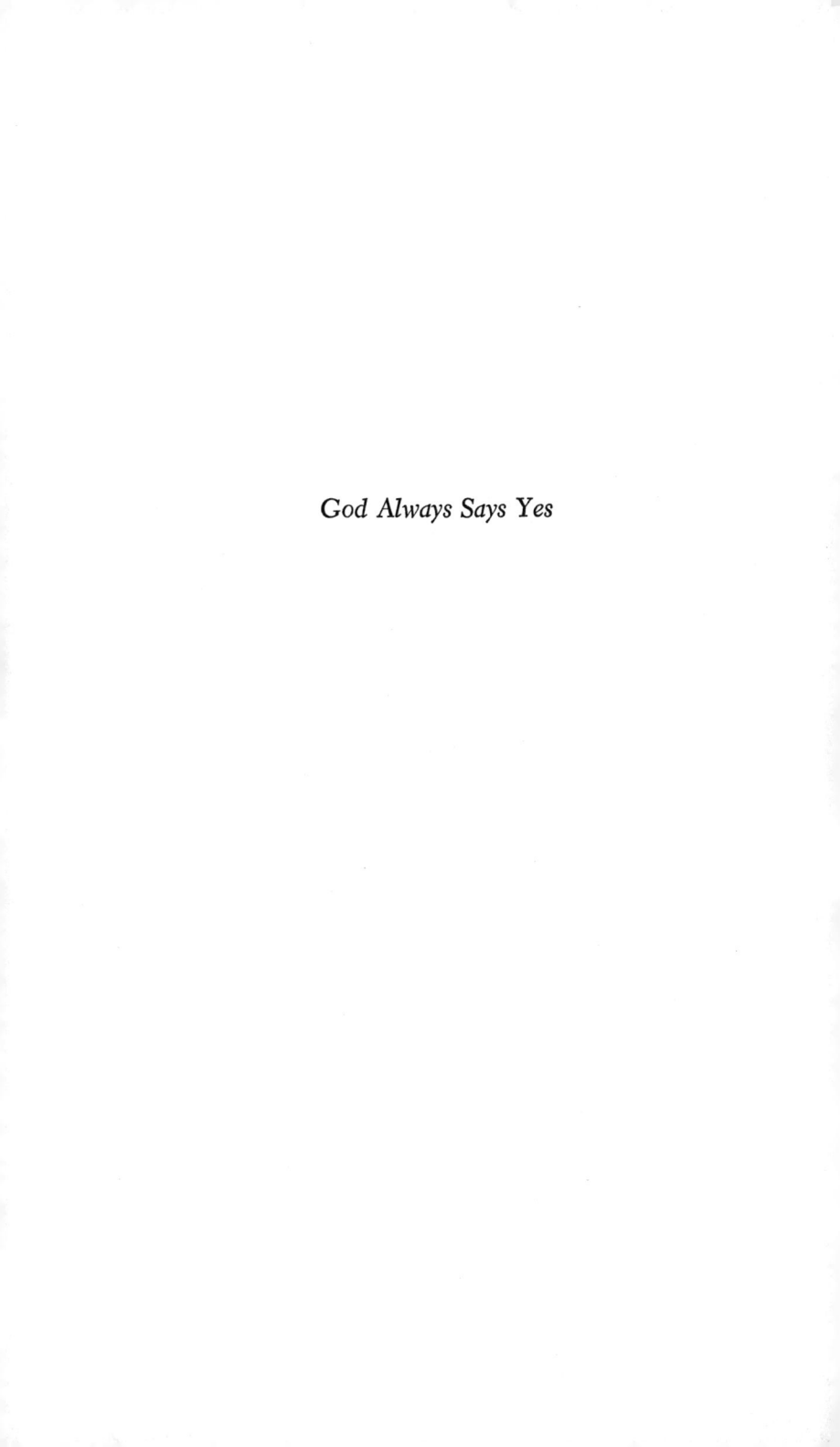

1. Crumbling Walls

What is happening to all mankind?

This is the question predominant in the minds and conversations of men and women everywhere today.

The invisible walls are crumbling. Man is finding himself. All mankind is being born again. All are coming into a new awareness of self.

We belong to the most exciting, most tremendous generation that has ever walked the earth. It is a generation that stands at a great spiritual crossroad. At this crossroad, we find a clear path—a path from which we cannot deviate, for it is our destiny.

To many, however, the path is overcast, overshadowed by old beliefs, as inadequate for meeting the challenges of today as the first airplane would be in this jet age.

What is happening? The shadows are being dispersed in the glorious light of Truth. This is our personal adventure today, more challenging and rewarding than any that science can envision in outer space. As science proceeds from proven facts, so does man as he embarks into the great, mysterious unknown—the kingdom within his own being.

There is a reason for everything under the sun. There is a sane and logical explanation of the most puzzling things in life. There is ground for, or a cause that confirms, every belief, and we all have the faculty of thinking consecutively and logically. For reasoning purposes, it is also necessary to have an open mind and heart so that we may understand, first ourselves and then others.

The inhabitants of the world of this particular time need to understand and honor each other. They must have unity, understanding. Of course, that unity need not be uniformity. We must have the power to communicate with each other. Communication is our greatest need today. To commune is to "put in common," and it must be "spirit to spirit" that communes, for the Spirit within is the only thing that is common to every human being. We have nothing to lose in understanding each other but everything to gain. Every man, woman, and child on the earth is a part of a whole expression that is called mankind.

In the past, man has dwelt in and stressed differences. Man has put the emphasis on separation, and thus invisible walls have been built. Generation after generation has been incapable of scaling the invisible walls of man's consciousness. These walls have been very strong, for the invisible is the greatest of all powers.

Finally these walls are crumbling and becoming as nothing. Since they have been the foundation of man's life, man is also crumbling. He is trembling and fearful, for he has lost his invisible support and, whether man understands it or not, he cannot stand or live without invisible support. The beliefs of man's mind, true or untrue, are what sustain him.

Man may deny the power of the invisible. He may say, "I shall always believe this; it was good enough for my father and grandfather, so it is good enough for me." *But* as he speaks "his house trembles," and the ground on which he stands is fast slipping away.

A new awareness is today permeating the consciousness of every living soul, even though at this time he is unconscious that it is the moving and pressing of an inner Spirit. Men are becoming aware of their true relationship to every other creature and of an ever-revealing awareness of something deep within their own being. This that is within is expanding momently, and it is demanding recognition.

Unconsciously, men are being drawn into a revelation and a knowledge of their relationship to the invisible power which is called God. Man is awakening to the supreme idea of the fatherhood of God and the brotherhood of man.

We look around the world and we see great divisions, strife, bitterness, race prejudice, differences of culture and customs. But all that we are seeing and hearing, all that is coming up at this time, is really the refuse, the rejected, worthless leavings, of an old regime. It is the end of that which can no longer rule. It is the outer proof of an inner change and an inner amalgamation that causes outer disturbances of old states of expression. If something tremendous were not happening, we would have no awareness of these things. They would not be surging up to be met.

WHO ARE WE?

Many times we have used the phrase "I was born." Perhaps we follow it with the name of the city or country in which we were born. One might say that he was born a Christian, a Jew, a Mohammedan, or a Buddhist. Or one might say that he was born Irish, French, Russian, or Chinese.

We may state that we were born in poverty or in riches,

on the wrong side of the tracks or in a mansion, but eventually *every* man must know that, primarily, he was born a son of God. When we accept the conscious realization of this truth we join the Transparent Race of God. The Transparent Race is the *one* that fills all; it is the innermost intelligence and life in every human form.

Let us leave the lesser and accept the greater. Let us leave separation and accept oneness.

To be born a son of God has nothing to do with the religion a man professes, for man's religion is incidental; usually, it represents the following of a pattern.

One question each of us must ask himself is: "Am I ready to accept myself as, and *be*, the son of God?" Are we ready to recognize all mankind as one brotherhood? Is there one father of us all? We belong to the great family of God, but do we know this, or are we unaware of and indifferent to our true selves? Have we forgotten our divine heritage?

When we look into the sacred writings of the world's religions, we find a variety of customs, many different languages, special terminology, but through it all there runs one golden thread—the continuing theme of the one Power.

It does not matter what we call this power—God, Allah, Brahma, Tao, or the Great Spirit of the American Indian—we find it in every religion. It is the common denominator of all life.

When we find this golden thread, we find God without beginning, God without ending, God filling man, sustaining him, and dwelling within him. There is no break in the chain of Truth. The eternal Truth of God's Presence underlies all that we call "differences." Tolstoy wrote, "There is a diversity of religious doctrines, but there is only one Religion."

There is only one Truth, though there may appear to be many. One person expresses it in one way and another person declares it in a different way. Man has many ideas about theology, creeds, dogmas, and rituals, but there is only one principle: the eternal presence of an unseen power. This unseen presence is in *you* today; it has always been in you and it will remain in you.

This One can do all things through you; you personally could not do them without the inner guidance and driving power. "I can of mine own self do nothing," said Jesus, but He also said, "With God all things are possible" (John 5:30; Matt. 19:26).

At this time every outer religion is pouring into this crossroad of all faith, emptying into one pure stream of life and truth, all to become one in a great mutual consciousness and awareness of God. As each comes and joins the throng, one more facet of the beauty and love of God unfolds before our eyes.

THE CROSSROAD OF UNDERSTANDING

As we stand at the crossroad of our mind and watch the differences move before us with the customs, the colors, the robes, the symbols, and the many interpretations of God, let us say, "How beautiful is the revelation of God in all people." We do not dwell on how different they are, but we are keenly aware of the various ways in which God expresses as man.

The differences we see must not make us doubt God, but they should bring us to a stronger conviction that God is the One, the only One, and has been that One always. Every religion comes to add its revelation to the already overflowing evidence of the one God.

Can we understand that it is God's plan that we are all different? Can we see the beauty of another person's way of expression?

I wonder if we are big enough for our time. For this is our challenge. Are we big enough for the age and revelation in which we live? Or do we still want to draw aside and say, "I am different. I am better. My way is the right way." Your way is only *the right way for you.*

The truth is that the golden thread is not only in all religions but also weaves its design through the heart and mind of every human being. *This one power and presence is the basis of all the religions of the world.*

Each man has the right to interpret this One as he pleases, to call it by whatever name satisfies him. We must know that no matter what he calls this power, how he interprets it, he is talking about *your* God and *my* God—the *Only* God. We have different languages, concepts, interpretations, and capacities, yet we all are expressing the One Spirit.

Religious differences are man-made, not God-made. The almightiness of Spirit and its expression in man is God-ordained and it cannot be changed.

If we go back to the Druids of ancient Britain and to the religious leaders of Gaul before the Romans came, we find they believed that everything—every hill, rock, tree, river, castle or cottage, every man, woman, child, animal—was inhabited by a Spirit. They believed that this Spirit was immortal.

Everything is moved by Spirit and is Spirit. God is, the Zend-Avesta says, "The Unconquerable One, The All-Seeing One, The All-Knowing One." The texts of Taoism say that God is "The Great Boundlessness, The Great Determiner, The Great Unity." And from Thrice-Greatest-Hermes come these words: "His Being is conceiving of all things and making them . . . for there is naught in all the world that is not He."

LOST IN DIFFERENCES

Does it matter that man accepts and describes his God in different ways? Does it matter how man believes, so long as it satisfies his soul and is the truth of God for him?

Do we understand that every man really believes in the "truth hidden for generations?" This is what every religion is seeking. Where has it been hidden?

It has been hidden in man's differences, in his different approaches and acceptances. The very truth was hidden because man could not reconcile these seeming differences. If we had been born in some other country, we too would be different. Our ideas would be different. Our ideas would also be different if we had been born in a different locale in the same country.

Does it make any difference how man explains it all to himself? What is the distinction if he believes in an invisible power that sustains him, and can come to know that the very life in his body is this power that is called God? Does his approach make any difference?

Man has been so mistaken in his beliefs about God, and so separated from God and so unaware of God's true relationship to him that every great religion strives to give God back to man, and man back to God. In the past, man has had the idea that God belongs only to the rich, the powerful, to the rulers and the holy men.

Jesus came to give God to the adulteress, the sinner, the thief, the liar, the wine bibber, and the ordinary man of the streets, as well as to the Scribe, the Pharisee, and the wealthy and powerful. He came to tell each man that no matter what he thinks about himself, the magnificent presence of God dwells within him.

It does not matter in what words man claims his oneness

with God. Isaiah says, "There is no God else beside me . . . for I am God, and there is none else (45:21–22)."

Jesus, when asked which is the first commandment of all, answered, "The first of all the commandments is, Hear, O Israel; The Lord our God is one Lord" (Mark 12:29). He took the words of the Mosaic law to tell us that there is only one God, only one presence and one power.

Does it truly matter whether it was Jesus who said, "The Kingdom of God is within you" (Luke 17:21); or Mohammed who said in the Koran, ". . . and the words of the Lord are perfect in Truth and Justice; none can change His words. He is hearing, knowing"; or whether it is in the Upanishads of Hinduism that it is stated, "The one God who is concealed in all beings, who pervades all, who is the inner soul of all beings, the Ruler of all actions, who dwells in all beings, the witness, who is mere thinking without qualities"?

Does it matter who expressed this truth? What really matters is that *we know it*, that there is only *one* Truth.

The truth of our oneness with God is in all teachings, *if you want to look*—and it is in your heart, *if you want to find it*.

As we stand at this spiritual crossroad, is our consciousness wide enough to see the beauty in every man's approach to God? Do we understand that everyone must express the truth of God in his own way?

Man cannot stand alone; he cannot exist safely without an understanding of something that supports him. Every man seeks in his own way and at his own level of consciousness for this Power that sustains him.

In truth there is only God. When we know the truth, there can no longer be divisions. God is the vitality, strength, and power in every religion. We do not know the "whole" about ourselves, but we are told that "it is given unto you to know" (Matt. 13:11).

The secret hidden for ages and generations has been given to us to know—to know that the flowing of all the differences of man are now uniting to become the truth of all men, the truth of God, and the revelation of God in His creation.

Do you feel separated from another who has a different way of praying? Many people have been taught methods of prayer that differ from ours. Does this make their God any farther away, any less able to answer prayer?

Do you know that this feeling of separation from others is sin? Sin is separation. So long as we separate ourselves from others in the sense that we feel we have a closer relationship to God than they have, our world will lie destitute. Every man walks with God in a path that God has chosen for this man. Let us *know* the truth that God is unfolding in and through His highest creation, man—every man, yes, every human being! This truth shall set us free.

Each man stands as a testimony to God. Be aware of the truth of God, for God is the power, the presence, the real in every Christian, Jew, Mohammedan, Buddhist—in everyone, everywhere.

Why do we close the doors of our mind to our brother and then build a world that we must share with him?

If you look at another and do not understand that other, say silently, "God made you. Why should I change you? We are spiritual beings, you and I, dwelling together in the harmony of Spirit. God made each of us in His own image and likeness, as He made all the different expressions of Himself on earth, each with its own inner image, each in the process of bringing forth the likeness of that image."

Let us accept the beauty of God's creation, the truth of all that He has made. Let us know that God is everywhere, evenly present, waiting for us to recognize and use His power. Let us know that this knowing will cause God to flood our lives.

This is *our age*. This is our accomplishment, *we are man!* No matter what our language, our customs, or our altar, we are here to bear witness to the truth that God makes His dwelling place in every man.

2. *The New Way of Life*

There is a new way of life in the world today. It is in the minds and hearts of mankind, but all men do not become aware of it at the same time. An awakening, or an awareness, takes place individually and almost without the person really knowing what is happening deep within.

This new way will take over the world. It will be a complete rearrangement of the essential principles and rules of life. This will affect every phase of man's being, from his physical health to his relationship with the universes in the farthest reaches of the sky.

The "old man" is outmoded; he will no longer be accepted or approved. He can no longer live in the changing world as he has lived in the world of the past; he must be refined, purified, and transformed into an unmixed state of being. This change is a cosmic change that makes him keenly aware of his relationship to the Creator of all and of his own part in the scheme of things.

All change comes first as an inner change. It usually manifests itself as a dissatisfaction with things as they are—an uneasiness, a discontent. These are always man's first signs of change and are not to be feared, but welcomed. There then comes a change of attitude in man toward himself, his fellow man, and toward those with whom he lives, both near and dear as well as far removed. This change extends to his very flesh, to every part and expression of his physical being.

Man must change. He knows he must, for, no matter what state of consciousness he is in, he is restless, never truly satisfied, always trying to alter himself and others as well as outside conditions and things. It is second nature for him to expect change, for change means exchange; each moment, each day, in life is exchanged for another; each phase of growth and unfoldment is change, for change is the master law of life.

Man is exchanging personality for individuality, fear for faith, indecision for stability, for he is coming to a new balance between his man-self and his God-self! God is the master word of today even though some men declare that God is dead. This is because God is so alive; only man's old conception of God is dead. Man's conception of a vacillating God of moods and hates and punishment is dead and gone; out of the ashes rises the true God, the God of principle, law, and life.

In the innermost part of man this change has already taken place. The inner working is being accomplished in each of us; otherwise we would not be so aware of the need for adjustment. The inner certainty is well established before there is any outer awareness. Just as desire for something is the thing itself in incipiency, so is our awareness of change a sign of growth and new spiritual unfoldment.

The souls of all men are feeling the pressure of the new way. All pressures and unrest in the world today are tokens of this great change. The pressures in man and outside him are the pressures of his new birth. We must be aware of what is happening to us so that we are not caught in the old concept of evil and punishment. We must *know* it signals a new birth and a new life.

Patience and strength are man's greatest virtues and needs at this moment of his unfoldment. It will take patience to keep our vision clear in the face of what seems to be a crumbling world. It will take patience to believe in ourselves as the foundations of the past slip and slide from beneath us. To be patient with yourself, your loved ones, your associates, and your new experiences will take much fortitude and forbearance. A patient person is one who endures "as seeing him who is invisible" (Heb. 11:27). This ability to see beyond what appears to be can be our greatest asset. Patience and the strength to stand in that patience is our goal.

THE FORGOTTEN SOURCE

In the past somewhere, sometime, or gradually over a period of time, man has lost the consciousness of his own indwelling power as an ever-present reality and force. Instead of receiving steady reenforcement from within, man has "forsaken . . . the fountain of living waters and hewed them out cisterns, broken cisterns, that can hold no water" (Jer. 2:13). Man has taken on states of consciousness based on the confusion of contradictory states of mind, and he finds himself running "back and forth." Now he must rise to the occasion and judge not from what he sees but from what he cannot see. We cannot accept the outer appearance as the real, but rather as "a cloud of unknowing."

The time has come for every one of us to be superhuman, because much is required of us. In truth we are superhuman. We have not touched the hem of the garment of our true power and authority as sons of God, for such we are and such we always have been, knowingly or unknowingly. We must recall our conscious mind to the truth that has always been and to the transformation that is taking place in each of us and in all humanity. We must awaken to our true potential.

We must be open from beginning to end, ready to be spent, like a river born in the mountain flowing to the sea, gathering from a thousand sources. We must open ourselves to the free flow of spirit and draw from spirit in all others, thus also gathering from a thousand sources.

We must be aware of our own inner essence, in which qualities inhere and ideas move. It is in and back and through all of us and everything. God is involved in all His creation as the essence, power, and presentation of all. We, in turn, create ourselves by evolving that which is involved in us—much as the butterfly is involved in the caterpillar and, by a secret process known only to God, evolves into a floating thing of beauty. We create our world of conditions and environment as well as our feelings and atmosphere much as a spider spins its world out of itself. We draw all things from invisible mind substance.

We draw from the invisible substance by thinking, feeling, and speaking. Do not underestimate your own spoken word and its power. It will be what we talk about that will manifest itself in our lives and make us able to do what we do. Let's remember this whether we understand it or not. There is a rule—a law of truth—and this truth is: The invisible substance of God lies back of everything and brings everything into manifestation, and it is moved by man's thought, his thought in action, which is his word and the essence of believing. Believing is the assurance and the acceptance of the soul!

WHAT MUST WE THINK?

What must we say and what must we believe? There are many levels of consciousness, so much to think, so much called good and so much called bad; there seems to be so many opinions, so much discussion, and so many conclusions. In reality, there is but *one* thing to believe and all else will fall into place: Believe that man and God are *one*. Believe that "there are diversities of operations, but it is the same God which worketh all in all" (I Cor. 12:6). God is the life and essence of you and of every other human being.

You are not one thing and God another; you, just where you are and as you are, are an expression of the one great Power. You may say, and believe, that you are a sick, poor human being, but fear, doubts, and inner struggles will fall away if you embrace this great truth that has always been since the beginning of time. Within each of us there is an inner realm heavily charged with ideas and with the power and energy to carry those ideas into outer expression. These ideas are for our use. Man has used them, is now using them, and by them he causes all manner of changes in his outer affairs, health, home, and relationships. The time has come when man must use his power for something far greater than just his outer comfort in this mundane world of affairs.

Man is losing contact with his life source, his spiritual energy, that which sustains life and balance. He is wasting the precious substance in his striving and too much seeking in the outer.

Economically, man is not sound and he is being forced to take a new look at things as they are and at himself. The whims of "labor" and "money" cause his affairs to fluctuate, and man is uncertain with a feeling that his roots are no longer there. Man has used his great mental-spiritual-physical power and created a world of things. People were made to love and things were made to use; but man is loving things and using people. Man is breaking the law of life. He has forgotten that this outer world is the expression of God's creative power through his own mind and feeling and for his use. All that man has and is, was and ever will be is coming forth from within his own being.

We have lost connection with spirit and we think of ourselves as something apart. We become so enthralled with this something that we become completely off balance. We forget our relationship with the whole and begin to withdraw from each other. We begin to make distinctions in what we call success and failure. We decide there are different kinds of people and become lost in duality. Soon we are involved in riches and poverty. Slowly we shut out everyone but a few chosen ones, and sometimes we finally let them go too. We find ourselves alone, not with God and inner peace, but with our outer concept of ourselves and our possessions and fears. But to be alone with nothing but material gain and prestige is a great emptiness.

LOST IN SYMBOLS

Money is a symbol of exchange and value. Money is only a tool—just a convenience. And yet we become slaves to it—a mere idea we brought forth to simplify life. Money was created as a means of achieving an end, and that end was meant for good. Money is not good or bad any more than a saw or hammer is good or bad. Money is a projection of the mind of man and receives all its strength from this source. If we were to become disinterested in money and not support it with our minds, it would disappear into nothingness.

In the new age and understanding, money will take its right place. It is an expression in man's God-mind created for the use of every man, but it becomes useless when it is not used for a good purpose.

Money is a powerful instrument for humanitarian and spiritual purposes and it cannot be diverted for too long from its true channel. It has been directed into channels of war and hate, and greed is the result of this misused power. There will be no peace and goodness in our world until man learns divine order in the use of money. Money stands between man and God.

Money and the material world that man has created will fail him. It is by failure that we learn what is true and eternal. Man and his soul and his source, God, are the world's true purpose. The world is for man; man is not a living sacrifice for the world—no, not any man.

Man must know himself. To know oneself is the final lesson for all mankind. When man decides to find out what is wrong with his world, he will find that *he himself* is what is wrong with his world. Man will discover that *he* is his world and that only he can change it. This is the cry of the man of old, "Repent," and to repent means to change one's mind. To repent means to rethink, and man has a great deal of rethinking to do.

The Great Intelligence only allows things to be mismanaged so long; in other words, God has no plan for man to destroy himself and man is being drawn up short for a day of reckoning. This lesson will be learned by every one of us. We will learn and make the adjustment, each in his own place of expression. We will learn in our own causes and effects. We learn, individually, in our own little world, in our own interests, and through the ones we love most. All true knowledge comes from our own experiences. We learn about every other life when it is our own that is involved. We learn about every man and his place when we must find our right and true place.

There is a Great Intelligence as well as the individual intelligence. Discipline is one of the great forces in the universe. Discipline is obedience to law and principle. God does not punish man, but breaking the law on any level has its repercussions; man is being driven back to his true and right expression. Man is now learning the law of his own source and supply and all of us are profiting by the experience.

TRUE EQUILIBRIUM

The lesson man is learning is balance. To balance is to stabilize, to poise evenly; it is the happy medium, the center path, the true human value. It is an equality between two things, and in our present day it is the balancing of accounts between the human and the divine. We are to bring these two into a state of equilibrium to make them, the human and the divine, equal each other. This is the inner, feeling soul-man, the invisible one, and the outer, doing, seeking, exploring visible man. *Man is balancing his invisible accounts in this day and time.*

We bring into being a wonderful world of things, houses, buildings, ships, and untold treasures, but we also bring forth the outer mental atmosphere, the surroundings, the environment, and pervading influences of love, hate, distrust, or faith-believing. We are the creator of war and every other form of evil also; man's mind is the womb of all that is in the world. We cause as we work with the Great Cause within. The time is at hand to look straight at our world and understand what causes it. Now is the time for each of us to shoulder our responsibility for things as they are. The law of God will not carry us any longer unless we do our part.

"I work and my Father works"—this was the keynote in the knowledge of the Master Craftsman of life.

Man has the tremendous power to bring ideas forth from the invisible realm of mind. Having done so, he has believed that that which was brought forth then belonged to him. This is true and not true—the divine paradox. When something is brought forth it belongs to all, for all minds are free to work upon it. It would have been rather silly to have invented an airplane and kept it in a cave. It is only in sharing that good comes forth for both the creator and the participant who is the sharer. There is an honor and a responsibility in such sharing.

The great financial structure in the world was built on a basis of mutual sharing. Man is learning that he cannot live alone, that he cannot have a corner on the world anywhere. The blackout in New York and the experience of being in it made it clear to my mind how much our life depends on others. Strangers are absolutely necessary to our life and well-being. How little we appreciate each other; how little we love the other person, the one who pulls the switch that lights our city, the one who turns the wrench to let the water through.

We are in the process of becoming aware of our own true self, and of the importance of everyone else in the world and the true value of every human being's relationship to every other human being. Our objective world has its source in the invisible, intangible mind of every man; each makes his contribution to the whole. We are all supposed to have the good that satisfies our needs. All desires are legitimate. All fulfillment should be an acceptance in our mind without question or fear. *Our good cannot come forth on any level except through our own mind and feeling.* If you would have your good in money or in any other form, you must be willing to release your mind from fear and limitation, not only for self but for all men everywhere. All poverty and lack are in consciousness and so is all abundance, with every man free to express and produce his own good.

We have had freedom of choice in our way of life, politics, social issues, and religion. In this freedom, we have diversified and now, in the new way of life, we are fulfilling the task of understanding, which brings about unification. We are learning the great lesson of detachment from personal privileges; we are learning to put the good of all before our own interests or the interest of any segment or particular group. We are finally coming back to the first Christmas message, "Good will to man—for *all men* always."

We each have our contribution to make to this new way of life and our greatest step forward now is readiness. Let us be ready for whatever lies ahead. The most important state of mind today is the ability to meet life where we find it. So, ask yourself a question: "How do I meet life?" When Hamlet was tricked by life, he said, "There's special providence in the fall of a sparrow. If it be now, 'tis not to come; if it be not to come, it will be now; if it be not now, yet it will come. The readiness is all."

Your readiness to meet life as it is and to know it for what it is, is your most important state of mind. You must know the great invisible power in the innermost part of your being is the great providence of God. This invisible mind-substance of which we are made and which we call consciousness extends throughout our whole being. In proportion as we know this shall we understand our relationship with God, and become a power on earth.

Do not get involved in making yourself over; just be your true self. A great change is in store for you; get ready, for it is good!

3. The Unfinished Story

There is an unfinished story, the story of every man's life. Man was created and brought forth to give an account of himself and to bring to completion his story.

The wisdom of God is manifested in and through man, and the unfinished story of man is called history. History is happening right now in every human being. This narrative is the unfinished story of God in man; and each man is moving through the experience of bringing forth and living his own part of that story.

"His-story" is man's story, and generation after generation write chapters in this story of man. I'm sure that if our great-great-grandfathers could walk through the world today, they would be amazed at the chapters that have been adding to the story.

This is the way it is with life—we never know what the next part will be or what will happen in the chapters to come. We do not know what may happen to us before this particular day is over, what great unfolding revelation, what outer material good may come forth for us. We say that a situation is hopeless or impossible, but tomorrow or next week it can be very different. We have encountered things we call final in our life, but there is nothing truly final. Everything is in the process of unfolding and change.

That everything will unfold to completion is the truth; the *way* is God's part, the *faith-believing* is our part. Every moment, every thought, every thing that concerns our life is part of the unfolding pattern of greater and greater good. Scripture tells us, "Eye hath not seen, nor ear heard, neither have entered into the heart of man, the things which God hath prepared for them that love him" (I Cor. 2:9).

It is a very strange thing about man's story—it is finished and then, again, it is not finished. If we think about the acorn that is going to be an oak tree, we know that in the acorn is every twig, leaf, limb, and the bark—even more acorns—of the tree; so, in a sense, it is finished. Yet the acorn is not finished. The activity of the law of God must move through this initial expression so that it may become in its outer form what it was created to be in its inner being.

This is the way it is with each of us. The divine pattern of God within us is finished because all that we are and can ever be is there within us, complete, else it could not be brought forth. In this sense we are finished, but, then again, we are not fulfilled. No matter where we are in life, what we are expressing, whatever condition or situation seems to be in our life and body, or in the life and body of someone we love, there is always another chapter; there is always something beyond. We cannot pause at any point in life and say, "This is it," because there is so much more.

Many of us do come to a point where we say, "This is it, this is failure, this is an incurable condition, this is a situation for which there is no answer"; if we accept this as true, from that time on we do not work on the finishing of our story. We stop there; we stagnate and reinfect ourselves. We renew the situation or condition that happen to be the part of our story at that point.

If we could only remember when we are meeting life, when there is loss of work or a physical challenge or some other experience that does not seem good, that it is but a stepping-stone to greater and greater good—if we understood this, we would find that our life would move forward.

Life may be measured by moments, hours, days, incidents, and experiences, but each page adds new highlights and new interests. At this point where we are now, we are telling the story of God with our lives.

You are interested in your story and I am interested in my story; this is as it should be, all of the thoughts of selfishness to the contrary. My responsibility is what I think and what I feel and what I do in my life. What you think, feel, and do belong to you.

Sometimes we get the idea that life is very dreary; that we are left out; that others are pushing ahead of us. But if we know that through God we are writing our story, then it is in our power to make life exciting and wonderful. We must learn to relax and enjoy each day of living.

As we ponder on these things, we come to a great truth: Everything, then, is passing. "It came to pass" are the words Luke used many times about many things. Our difficulty is that we are not able to let things pass. We hold on to them; we clutch them to us with our hearts and minds.

We should learn the secret of letting go, for whatever is happening to us right now will pass, if we let it, and that which is to come after it will begin to unfold the next chapter in our story.

There are a few chapters in the Bible that are rarely read. These are the "begats." They read, "So-and-so begat so-and-so, and so and so begat . . ."; then all is begotten, all is caused, every effect is produced. There is a great secret in the "begats" because one experience, one feeling, one state of mind begets another and what follows begets the next. Therefore, how we meet each life experience begets the next experience, the next series of incidents.

We must let these states of consciousness unfold in us easily, because unfold they will in spite of us, and any attempt to hold life back causes pressure. We cannot truly hold back life for we cannot help living and growing; we can only burden and torment ourselves.

If we do not take everything as it comes in our stride, life has a strange and mysterious way of causing us to take the steps in spite of ourselves. These steps are wonderful, and although we sometimes find them hard to take, beyond each and every moment we live is a higher and greater good. As we take the steps of life some of them do not seem good to our human thinking; nevertheless, all of them lead directly to our completion and fulfillment.

LIFE IS A PROCESS

Let us remember the seed that drops into the ground. The shell of the seed must fall away to let the shoot come up so that there may be fruition. So, in the experiences of our life, the shell of our consciousness (what we have believed, thought, felt) begins to fall away so that the unique and beautiful thing that is within us may come forth.

When we think about ourselves and the world around us, we realize that God does not give us anything that is finished. The baby isn't finished, the child isn't finished, and the man isn't finished, either. There is a development taking place in each human being right now, a process that cannot be fathomed. There is great advancement in the world at this time. Growth and unfoldment has been stepped up. We are not yet fully what God has created us to become, but we are on our way and where we are now is wonderful.

We are the witnesses and the partakers of a dying consciousness and of the birth of a new way of life. We are feeling the death pangs and the labor pains at the same time. We may still cling to some very dark spots in history and in our personal chapters of life, but we have the capacity to become great enough and free enough to move along with the story.

No moment, however low or however transcendent, can deter our advancement. Even in God's time, we can only stand still for the moment; then we must press on. We must move on with the story. The past will take its place in time. No matter what the past has been, no matter how much bloodshed, hurt, unhappiness, and anxiety man has experienced, it is part of the story. In each chapter is beauty and wonder, and we find it is the purpose of life.

We must learn to live each day. We cannot go forward if we insist on carrying with us the whole past of mankind, still less our own individual past. Learn the wonderful secret of letting the days pass—letting the past pass. Let us leave the past safely in God's hands so that our life will be free to unfold.

The world and everything in it is in the process of unfoldment and change, of being completed and of beginning again. The seed is not the tree—we know that—yet in essence it *is* the tree. Essence means to be. The seed is the tree to be. We are God in essence, God to be.

The gold is in the earth, but man must find it. The electricity is in the ethers and man has captured it and led it to do the things it can do. The atomic power has always been in the invisible, and man has always, unknowingly, used it. To *use* a substance is the process of finishing it.

The atomic power is the constant movement of spirit, even

in your smallest finger, and it fills your body and all of the world. We may call it by various names, but science is proving it basically to be the only power in the universe—the power of the invisible ethers as well as the visible expression.

MAN IS THE FINISHER

The mystery of God is in man's mind and heart, and he is in the process of unfolding it. Man is the finisher of that which is never finished and yet which is finished. Let us think about this paradox. Man is the finisher of that which is never finished, that which never can be finished because it merges and becomes something else. As soon as we think we have finished anything, we begin again. This is good because to finish means to limit, and there is no limit to God. There is no limit to God, and therefore no limit to us.

Since there is no limit to you or to me or to our capacities, let us throw off all limiting thoughts and beliefs. Let us stop saying that this or that is all we can do or as far as we can go.

If the story is to go on, we must recognize that we are limitless. There is discouragement sometimes. Things drop out of sight and seem to end, but if we stand still, they will reappear. Remember the wonderful words of Jesus in the Gospel of Thomas: We must stand at the beginning, He said, and know what the end will be. It is not given to us to know what is in-between—only as it is revealed to us moment by moment. God lives in us, the finished creation that is in the process of unfoldment.

God works in man in three ways. He creates, provides, and redeems. He is the great providence of man, providing and exercising on our behalf foresight, guidance, and loving care.

When we hear the word "redeem," we think of the old ideas of sin and evil, but redeem means much more than that. When the seed is planted in the earth and unfolds, it redeems the pattern that is within it and completes it. To redeem is to bring the image that is within into outer reality. God is creating and *now* providing as he redeems each of us.

We do not always believe this because we feel anxiety and worry about our families, fear of old age, and many other accepted, untrue ideas. As a result, we are receiving what we do not need or want because we are accepting it with our thought and feeling.

God is the All-Provider—let Him provide. We are given the days of life to live, love, and enjoy. We should not spend the power of mind in useless fear and worry about the future nor anticipate terrible experiences that can or might happen to us or our loved ones. God is the dearest and deepest desire of every man's heart because God is yearning *as* us, as well as *in* us and *through* us.

When we think of the fulfillment of God, we sometimes think of clothes, houses, opportunities, and health but the fulfillment of God can only be found in the yearning of our heart, not in material things. God is yearning in each of us and this yearning must be satisfied. It is a longing that must be given expression. As we accept the yearnings and desires of our innermost heart, we are touching the invisible essence of God—that which we are to be.

OUR TRUE VOCATION

The law or pattern of God is yearning in each of us right now, for all yearning is God. The essence within you is not just a need of this day; it is omnipresent and universal.

We think of our outer work as our vocation, but man truly has but one vocation—to develop and bring forth his God-self. Every other work is an avocation, a minor occupation, that calls us away from our *true* work.

Your true vocation is releasing and fulfilling your soul.

My true vocation is releasing and fulfilling my soul. If we do not do this, we become sick inside—sick with a feeling of incompletion and emptiness that beats within us all the time. It becomes such an emptiness gnawing within that we cannot keep our mind clear to do the things that would fulfill our soul.

Let us pursue our true vocation for which we were created. We must become aware of the unfolding pattern of life, knowing that no matter where we are today, there is another moment, another day.

There is always another chapter to this great and wonderful story. The truth of this unfinished story is that you have never failed, that you cannot fail.

Man thinks he can fail; man thinks he is failing; man thinks he has failed. Man thinks others are failing and that others have failed him. This is *not* true. What we have called failure is but the unfolding experiences that have brought us to this present time.

To us, many things are discouraging simply because they have not turned out the way *we planned them*. We have setbacks, but in each one God is saying, "This is not the way; this cannot lead you to your good."

If you find yourself in a dead-end street, you know that you must turn about and retrace your steps. This is the way it is with life.

We all have periods when we give up to thoughts of failure. If you are entertaining such thoughts right now, go back to the time you think you failed. Go back in your mind, for only in your mind can you reach it. All failure is in mind. Now, turn about and understand that there is only one way for you and that way is forward. God created you to unfold. In you He is unfolding, providing, and opening up the way for you to complete each chapter of your story.

Let us remember Joshua, the successor to Moses, and the

words that the Lord spoke to him: "There shall not any man be able to stand before thee all the days of thy life: . . . I will not fail thee, nor forsake thee. Be strong and of a good courage . . ." (Josh. 1:5–6).

But Joshua, like each of us at times, "rent his clothes, and fell to the earth upon his face," and asked why. Why did this happen? Why? The Lord said to him, "Get thee up; wherefore liest thou thus upon thy face?" (Josh. 7:6, 10). In other words, the Lord was saying, "I can't help you as long as you are lying on your face. Get up and I will help you." Jesus told us there is man's part and God's part. Man's part is to stand upright, to "seek . . . first the Kingdom" (Matt. 6:33), to walk like a son of God. Everything will then be revealed to him that he needs to know.

So, each step will be taken for you, if you will get up and face it. "On your face" means that you are not facing it. Get up in consciousness and face what has been called failure, incurable conditions, impossible situations. Thousands of men and women have proved that what we call incurable is curable, that what has been termed impossible is possible.

The promise of God is that He will sustain you, pour out His good upon you, and fulfill you if you will get up and try again. These times of difficulties and disappointments, when everything seems to come to a standstill, are but changes in tempo, changes of pattern, or changes of some other kind. These changes are always the new chapter.

We must know that God is with us, sustaining us, and that He cannot fail us because, as He has said, "there is none else, there is no God besides me: I girded thee, though thou hast not known me" (Isaiah 45:5).

If we can undergo every examination—and every experience is an examination—to see if we remember that God is here, there, and everywhere, then we have progressed.

Can we pass the test that everything is good? Perhaps not without trembling, but trembling or not, let us be confident that all is well.

Pray, always, that you may listen and respond to all that God would do through you, even though you may be walking through what seems to be loss of material good, loss of position, loss of faith, loss of loved ones. Know that you cannot lose anything that is in your heart. All of God, all good, and all there is, is in your heart.

As we continue to realize our own unfinished story, let us not blame our experiences on other people. No one else is responsible for what may be happening to us, for we are our own world.

As we look at the state of affairs in the outer world, let us not blame situations on our environment. We are the creator of our environment, and there can be nothing except what we choose. *This is the secret of the mind* and the realm of accepted thoughts whether they are true or untrue.

Do not blame situations or conditions in your life on anyone else, but take time to examine your own mind; you will find the secret of life, the source of all, within.

Do not blame your forefathers, for you can only inherit states of mind, not weaknesses.

Do not blame things on your loved ones, but know that you are writing your own story, either with clear knowledge of the unfolding God-presence or without this knowledge —which in this case would be working without proper tools.

Ernest Wilson says in his book *Sons of Heaven* that "we are all sons of heaven, wandering in a strange country, homesick for our God-self, our true-self." It does not matter how much money we have or how brightly fame and fortune smile upon us; we all have this longing to go home—to enter a place within ourselves where we are completely balanced between the physical self and the invisible spiritual being that dwells within each of us.

Let us recognize that the promises in Scripture are sure. We can depend upon them, for they were meant for us regardless of our past circumstances or behavior or the appearances of today. The moment you use a principle, it will work for you whether it is a principle of mathematics or of the mind.

Through the power within us, we can do all things. We are writing our own story and it is a tremendous story. We not only write it, but we are also required to live it.

Let us move out into today, tonight, tomorrow, and the days that will follow, knowing that the point where we are is never the end. There is always greater and greater good unfolding, but it cannot be reached unless we press forward.

Ernest Wilson
—Son of Heaven

4. The Law of God Is Completion

Why is my life empty? Why do my struggles come to naught? Why do I always fall short of my goal? Why, even though I have found fame and fortune, is my soul hungry and unsatisfied? Why am I, in my own estimation, a failure? Why am I unloved and alone? Why can't I love more, give more, and why does it seem that my hands are always tied? Why can't I trust people and be free and happy? Why do I go about day after day, pretending, smiling, trying to belong, when my heart and soul feel like ice? Why am I lonely in a crowd? Why, when I have planned my life so carefully and brought it to a satisfactory place, am I haunted with unrest and a sense of something unfulfilled? Why, O God, *why* do I not have what is mine?

The heart of man cries out for satisfaction and fulfillment. Every creation of God came into being for the sole purpose of unfolding into full expression; each came to fulfill a destiny. This expression of God is to be perfect. Why, then, is this not accomplished? Why is the world full of frustration, neurosis, and hopelessness? Where is this perfect world that we hear so much about? Sometimes we hear so much about it that, taunted by the seeming emptiness of our own life, we rebel at words that sound false. Yet, in our own hearts we know that something has escaped us, and we strive to find this perfection.

The reason there is an unanswered cry in the heart of man is very simple: Man himself omits doing something that is necessary to his own fulfillment. Everything God created is under the Law of Life, yet man does not know the simple laws that govern him. He will not understand life, nor will he have his good consistently until he knows the Law and does something about it!

In the Gospel of Thomas, Jesus says, "Give the things of Caesar to Caesar, give the things of God to God, and give Me what is mine." Even when we have so much, or so little, our hearts still say, "Give me what is mine!"

Thomas also says, "How much will you bear?" To bear means to bring forth. How much longer before you bring forth? How much longer will it be? When are *you* going to *do* something about your life? For you, and you alone, can solve the mystery of life for yourself.

Usually, when we want to achieve something we must take into account the cost, the effort, and the place we must go to accomplish the thing desired, but this is not so with *true* growth and development. To turn within to your own heart and mind is no distance at all, and there is no cost. You must simply shut the door of the outer self with all its striving and struggling; then sit quietly for a few moments at a time and not even think of how, or when, or why. This takes a little practice, for it is like putting aside your outer garments and allowing your body to relax and breathe. It means putting aside your outer world and letting your soul be free and filled with *true life*. This is meditation.

There is no excuse for anyone to have an empty life. Life

is to live; there is a right and perfect way to live and we must find that way. *Perfection is not a goal but an unfolding, and this unfolding is the purpose of all life!* True living is never surface living; rather, it takes place deep within us. Today, exactly where you are, you possess the key to the puzzle of life and the answer to every problem. Why not do something about it? Do IT NOW!

We have believed that we must accept the opinions and conditions of the outer world without question, but in this very belief lies slavery. Do not blindly follow anyone or accept everything you hear as gospel truth, especially when this blind acceptance leaves you empty within and unsatisfied. If you do not have peace, power, and a measure of contentment in your life, you have departed in some way from the Law of Life or you have not yet found it. Do not go back to try to find where you turned off this path of *true life*. Do not waste time in vain regrets. Forget it—forget the past *now!* Open your mind and heart to that great Power within you whose sole purpose is to take care of you. This Power is the Law of Life; the ever-renewing, unfolding, vitalizing Power within you—this power is God! You have depths of strength and vitality you have not yet tapped. Begin again and live again that you may know why you are here and what you are to accomplish.

The Law of Life is as old as time, as new and vibrant as today, as usable as an automobile and as necessary as our breath. What man has called God is actually the Law of Life! Man has been afraid of the word God. Either he has held it in awe and reverence or he has ridiculed the idea of something he could not comprehend or see. To man, God has not been a practical, workable, close, or warm power, but only a word to be talked about or feared. We have been afraid of becoming entangled in a relationship with God that might keep us from self-expression, that might steal away our good, our loved ones, or even our own life. We have not known the true nature of God and we have avoided what we could not understand. We have been unaware of the very secret of the universe, the law of our own life.

God is the science of knowing the movement of the universe, the only Presence in all and through all, no matter by what name we call this Presence. God is that which moves everything, that which even at this moment is moving, breathing, thinking, knowing, and feeling in the midst of *you!* God is the urge within you that leads you on; that which makes you dissatisfied with things as they are, so you may have more of the real things of life. Let us know about the laws that express this mighty Power that fills us all.

THE LAW OF RELATIVITY

The first law to be considered is the Law of Relativity. Everything visible anywhere in the universe is relative to something that is invisible. Everything that you are, or could ever be, is caused by the unseen Presence, the faceless, formless something we roughly call life, eternally present, yet unseen, within our own being. All that is seen is related to the unseen, and the unseen is always there. This is the greatest truth man can know, the greatest truth on earth. We are never alone; a mighty power called God is our counterpart, our unseen self. When you look at another human being (or at yourself) you should know that the unseen Presence is there, just as simply as you look at a tree and know that its roots are deep in the earth and that sap flows through its system. The sap is unseen, yet you know the tree could have no life without this hidden essence. As you look at a man, you should know that the unseen Presence walks with him, talks in him, moves in him, and truly *is the man.*

So, everything in life—good or what we are so apt to call

bad—is held by the invisible cord of the mind. All conditions, situations, health or lack of it, happiness or bondage, have their source within us, in our minds—to each his own. Therefore, this being true, we have dominion and authority over our own body and affairs. We each hold the key to ourselves. Are we willing to know the truth about ourselves? We *do* want to be healthy, free, and happy, don't we? In the past we have blamed environment, parents, the times, opportunities or lack of opportunities, or other people for the flaws in our condition, when all the time the real cause lies *within us*.

There is something we do not know, understand, or do, but it is something we are all capable of knowing, understanding, and doing. Inscribed upon the ancient Delphic oracle were these great words: "Know thyself." And Shakespeare said, "To thine own self be true. . . ." So, you must know the truth about this self and that "truth shall make you free." If you would be true to yourself today, stop blaming things that are disrupting your life on someone else or on something outside yourself. Here is the secret of all secrets: Acknowledge your power to bring upon yourself the unhappy, unfortunate things; then *you will automatically accept the power to bring into your life whatsoever you really need*. In your mind is the invisible source of all achievement. Accept the challenge of your own responsibility and you will change the image and expression of your life. "As a man thinketh in his heart, so is he."

THE LAW OF VIBRATION

Modern scientists have discovered a law that stems from antiquity. This is the Law of Movement, or Vibration. Nothing is static, nothing truly rests; everything moves or vibrates. This is the constant life, animation, and activity of all creation. All things are moving, even though they appear to be at rest. Ice, water, and steam are the same substance at different rates of vibration. Man's rate of vibration is raised or lowered by his state of mind. Changes in man's mind or consciousness mean changes in body and affairs. The action of the mind makes definite changes in the body. Fear causes us to be "frozen in our tracks," seemingly paralyzed or "glued to the floor." We have different reactions to different states of mind—we can blush, break into cold perspiration, or be nauseated because of our own thoughts and feelings. It follows, therefore, that the action of our mind can also heal our bodies and set us free to do the things we really desire to do.

When we discover the Law of Vibration, we have touched the seat of power. The Law of Vibration sets us free from condemnation and criticism of the past, even from the belief in "good" and "evil." We are growing and unfolding so fast that we are not the same persons we were yesterday or the day before. Tomorrow we will not be what we are today. We are not capable of expressing in the same way; consequently, *we cannot accept any condition or situation as permanent or incurable!*

If fear thoughts cause actual physical changes as the vibrations of the body are *lowered*, then thoughts of hope, peace, strength, and power, by *lifting* the vibrations of the body, can also bring about physical changes. This very moment, as you read and fill your mind with these truths, your whole being is filled with Spirit as you are set free from old fears and beliefs of failure and guilt. No matter what the condition in your body or the situation in your life seems to be, *it will pass*, for this is the Law of Vibration. As you raise the vibrations of your mind and body by refusing to accept a situation, by either ignoring it or not caring about it, you will find, strangely enough, that you have escaped the consequences. By your refusal to accept that which is not good, you set free the natural action of good within you. This is healing. This is the action of God.

Do not give the creative power of your mind to any condition or situation that you do not want in your body, life, or world. Do not give your attention to things that cause you to be fearful, not even in the attempt to make things "right." Know that the Law of Vibration will set you free. As surely as any situation or condition has come into your life, it must pass. This is the flow of life, for life flows on and on. You are not the person you were a day ago, or even an hour ago. Do not hold fast in your mind to any state of being, whether you call it good or not good, no matter how much it may dominate your life. Lend your self, your life, and your mind to the ever-flowing Law of Life and Movement.

You steal away your own life and joy, you ruin your own health and interfere with your human relationships by your great concern over things that seem to be in others or in the world about you, and by your own great desire to change these things in the "outer." *You do not or cannot change anything outside your own mind*; the great Law of Vibration, of change and growth, is written in the center of every living thing. All change proceeds outward from within. Lincoln said, "A man can no more change himself than he can lift himself by his boot straps." All change comes from within. If we would let the Law of Vibration carry us forward, if we would quit striving, arranging, and rearranging, and just STAND STILL in our mind and wait upon the action of God, we would find new and wonderful things moving into our lives both inwardly and outwardly. Remember, nothing is permanent; nothing is incurable. There is no failure. Nothing is impossible. All things are passing ever upward and onward. Practice letting things *pass*, by refusing to sustain them. All power has been given to you. *Use it!*

THE LAW OF POLARITY

There is still another universal law that is important in the life of man. This is the Law of Polarity. Everything has its two poles, its two extremes, its two opposites. All is dual. Opposites are identical in nature but different in degree. Seed, root, blossom, and fruit are different degrees of the same creation. Extremes meet: high and low, north and south, hot and cold—Where does the darkness end and the light begin? If one travels far enough north, he will find that he is traveling south. How far can a boy run into the woods? asks the old riddle. The answer is: Only halfway, for after that he is running *out* again. If we travel far enough in fear and anxiety, we will find ourselves traveling in faith. When we find ourselves at the very bottom, there is only one way to go—*up!*

Good is not one thing and bad another. There are simply different degrees of good: less good or more good. Man is physical and spiritual; these are different in degree but identical in nature, like hot and cold, young and old. The only difference between the young and the old is that the young have come lately, the old have been here longer. Where does one thing end and another begin? They don't; they are merging, for they are both the same, two stages of the same thing. There is large and small, hard and soft, sharp and dull, like and dislike, love and hate, poverty and plenty, giving and receiving; there are two sides to everything. Both are true —with countless degrees in between.

All paradoxes can be reconciled. Man can move from one extreme to another and both are God. The secret of life is that man has the power to play the music of life on the scale between the poles. Man can transmute any condition into its own opposite.

Love is not diametrically opposite to hate. Man can change hate into love, fear into courage, laziness into activity, sickness into health, dislike into like, or vice versa. All these so-called opposites are different degrees of the same thing. If we believe that sickness is one thing and health another, and that it is impossible to change one into another, then everything seems hopeless. But, when we understand that these are different degrees of the same thing, what was impossible becomes possible. We simply slide our thoughts along the scale between the poles of the mind to a greater degree of health, abundance, or whatever it is we need to change. The sliding scale upward is simply moving from *knowing less* to *knowing more*, or being *conscious of more*.

All polarization in the human being is in mind. When we change our moods, our attitudes, our outlook on life, our feelings about ourselves and others, we raise the vibrations of our mind, we change our polarity; we do this degree by degree. As we turn our mind toward the opposite of any condition, we automatically slide along the scale of life to the higher (or lower) pole.

To truly pray is to use the law of polarity. Prayer is praise, thus lifting the mind from fear, separation, censure and condemnation to oneness, sameness and completion. Begin now to use the Law of Praise (Prays). As you praise your body, or whatever the situation in your life, you change the pole of your mind and discover the law of answered prayer. The Law of Polarity is simple and natural; it is simply changing degrees of expression. The Law of Polarity sets you free from the incurable, the impossible. You cannot transmute something into a thing that is entirely different, but you *can* change the degree of the same thing. No matter what the setback, failure, or condition, it is in your domain. You have the authority to raise the vibration and polarize your mind to any degree of expression. Remember: *YOU have the power, and only YOU can move your mind.*

All things that have seemed impossible become possible through polarization. Why be a slave to conditions, situations, and diseases? Why be sick and poor? We do not need any special kind of salvation or long-drawn-out making amends with our God; just as we are today, we ourselves are all-power. We can do anything that is needful to change our lives with this power that is ours. We always have the choice, either to be overwhelmed by the world and the conditions in it, or to take our own God-given power and *use it*. *Use* is a simple and tremendous law of life. *Use* is the Law of Polarity. You have the power and ability to change any condition, but you, and you alone, must use the Law for yourself.

THE LAW OF RHYTHM

Scientists have found the Laws of Relativity, of Vibration, and of Polarity, and *all of these* are caught up in a divine rhythm. To understand the Law of Rhythm is to be free from anxiety and worry. In everything in the universe, and in man, there is a measured motion, to and fro, up and down, backward and forward, ebb and flow. God's Law of Life is based on rhythm. There is always action and reaction, advance and retreat; we take a breath and we let it go. Our every step is rhythm. The heart beats with the rhythm of God. Man does not understand how success is followed by failure, or how peace of mind and faith in God can be his, then apparently slip away. Man tries many schemes to neutralize and annul the principle of rhythm, but he cannot because rhythm is the law of growth and unfoldment. The bud that will be the new leaf in the spring pushes forth far enough in the autumn to loosen the old leaf so that it may fall and make way for the new. It is always the invisible action of the new that causes us to let go of the old. Why will we not let go joyfully so that the new growth may come forth?

On the staff of Life, the great melody is played between the two extremes and these extremes are always with man. When man understands the Law of Rhythm, he no longer condemns himself and wastes his life searching for the cause of everything that has happened to him. The rhythmic swing of the pendulum is ever in evidence and it accounts for the moods, feelings, and many perplexing states of mind we experience. When we reach a low point, this is an indication that the swing upward must surely follow. We stand on the beach and watch the tide go out; if we stand still and wait, we will see it flow in again. If the universal pendulum appears to be at a standstill in your mind and heart, do not panic, do not give up, do not be thrown by moods, feelings, or other changes in your life, for that pendulum will swing back again. If you are at a low point physically, in finances, in your contribution to the world, in prestige, in human relationships, learn the secret of rhythm! *Nothing can be lost.* The ebb and flow goes on around us, in business, in love, and in every human relationship. Do not be affected by the inflow or the outflow. Nothing is taken except something be given in return; the measure of the swing to the left is the measure of the swing to the right.

There is something in every challenge, every low period, that gives the lift. The harder the ball strikes, the higher it bounces. Do not be afraid of hitting the bottom, for the harder you hit, the higher you will go upward. When you find yourself at lowest ebb, do not give up and stay there. Lift your mind and look for the change upward that is sure to come. Expect a change for the better because it is inevitable—it is the Law—but you must look for it and expect it. Hopelessness is like quicksand, so don't be caught in it. Your good will compensate for or counterbalance all that seems bad in your life. All that seems the opposite of good *is* good, so wait for the flow, for the swing of the pendulum. There is nothing to fear, nothing to dread, for nothing is final—the Law is constant.

The most discouraging experience, the most dreadful thing in your life, has behind it some great good. Look for the return of good in greater measure. Man believes in endings but there is never an end of anything, only the beginning of something greater and higher. What man calls an ending is the movement away from something that has served its purpose, that is outgrown, so that that which is ready may come into expression. This is the constantly unfolding Law of Life. Nothing can stand still; we ourselves would not want life to stand still. Life without change causes man to come to a state of boredom—the boredom that is the nemesis of all growth.

THE LAW OF GENDER

The greatest of all the laws of God is the Law of Gender. It is through this law that every living soul has made entrance into a living body, and by this same law man brings his outer world into visibility. Everything we have in our life—and affairs—is here now because we have used the Law of Gender. We were all conceived, nourished through gestation, and born into a physical being. This is the creative power of God at work. Except through the seed, the shoot, the tree, the leaf, the blossom, the fruit, there could be no expression of nature. *There is no other way.* Except through the Law of God, nothing can come forth. The Law is: As above, so below. Man, being a creator, carries the creation forth in his body, world, and affairs. Creation is *never done* and over with; it goes on and on.

A child is not created and that is it; the infant comes from the embryo, the child from the infant, the adult from the child. The infant does not die to become the child, nor does the child die to become a man. It is the law of creation that is carried on in living! The basic physical being is the outer shell or expression of the soul. The living human being carries on this creation after the same plan as the Creator.

At every level of expression the Law holds true; therefore each thing that man brings forth in the "outer" must follow the same basic law: Each thing must first be conceived in the womb of man's mind, *be nourished by the Spirit and by the conscious awareness of man's own faith-believing*. It is then brought forth into fulfillment. We must understand our role in the great plan of creation. Creation is not done and finished; it continues on and on, progressing from "glory to glory." The past was a former creation, like our first attempts to coordinate our hand and mind in writing. The present is *being* created and is subject to change and improvement.

There are two distinct parts in man that carry on this creation: the thinking part and the feeling part. For every conception these two *parts* must make union. Man must accept in his mind, and what he has accepted in mind he must feel with every fiber of his being. Until this happens, man has not conceived; he is only talking or thinking about what might be—what could be. Thinking or talking is not enough. The thing to be created and brought forth must be overshadowed by a feeling so great that the whole soul is athrob with it. Many plans and dreams in our soul do not come forth into our life because we lack this divine ingredient—*feeling*.

We must feel deeply if we are to bring forth. Surface feelings make empty lives. Man is not in earnest about his role of creator; he is lackadaisical, halfhearted—he has not kindled the "fire of God" without which nothing can be consummated. If there is to be completion and achievement, there must be no part lacking. The law must be fulfilled in its entirety.

To fulfill our destiny we must stir up the great fire of God which is Love, an ecstasy of joy and rapture that is pure *knowing* and *completion*. To develop and draw forth out of our being the great Power that consummates all things, we must talk about this power and think about it and know that it is the power that man has called God. Similarly, on the level of expression, we must talk about good, think about good, and expect good—that good will fill our life, body, and affairs. We must woo good if we would have good. We must diligently *perform* the Law of Life if we would fulfill the Law of God.

In the beginning, we were created perfect and placed in a perfect setting. Our expression is an ever-flowing and moving universe of light and activity, and we are equipped with all power to carry on God's creation. Man's own failure is in the continuing process—in not being a free channel for his own God-feeling. Man has developed lopsidedly. He thinks too much without feeling deeply and he has become sterile. Man must return to his perfect purpose: the bringing forth of his perfect God-pattern and God-expression by the completion of his thinking mind and his feeling soul. He must use the Law of Gender.

If man cries out, "Give me what is mine!" then man must comply with the Law, because it is impossible to receive anything outside the Law. Man, being a son of God, must take what is his if he is to have it. Man must think, but he must also feel. Thinking and feeling must have equal exercise and be accorded equal honor.

Go deep within yourself—tap the hidden, invisible resources within. Learn to feel again and you will find that you live again. Wherever you are today, *get up* and begin again. You need not be barren, empty, ineffective, useless, unfulfilled. The Law of Life is *completion*. What is yours is for you, but you must do your part. *Now is the time to start—bless you on your way.*

> Awake up
> Get up — Law Pendulum
> Keeps up Belief / Faith

5. The Untouchable You

Are you an inhabitant of the age in which you live? Do you know that you belong to a new and wonderful world? The old world is dying and a new world is being born. We are the in-between generation. Man is on his way back to God, to an awareness of an invisible essence in him that is All-Good. He is traveling fast and light; he is on his way back to himself.

We are a part of two worlds. These are two distinct states of consciousness: the old consciousness of fear, sin, hate, and unhappiness; and the new realization of faith in God, oneness with God-self, right relationships with one another, and a happy life of adventure and fulfillment. There is much pressure in our world today from these two states of consciousness—one pressing from within man, the other pressing from the "outer."

We are conscious of the sorrow or death pangs of the old dying state of consciousness and of the labor pains of the new consciousness that is being born. In the old dispensation, man believed that both his "evil" and his "good" came

> John 8:32
> The truth is within every man - and man must turn back within himself and find it for himself

from outside himself, and that over this he had little or no control.

In the new expression, man must go where his good is. Man must go within his own being to find the answer to all that he is or can ever be. Man must look to himself because the hope of the world is in man's own being. "You shall know the truth and the truth shall make you free" (John 8:32). The truth is within man and every man must turn back within himself and find it for himself.

The secret of man's life lies in the invisible—the invisible that the scientist explores and the invisible that is the peace and presence of God. The scientist has found that nothing is lost, that all things only change form. The religionist knows that there is only God, the visible and invisible, and that there is no extinction—only transformation. "Be ye transformed by the renewing of your mind" (Rom. 12:2).

Man, on the long road to self-discovery, has made a circle and is coming back to face himself. God in man is not a new idea; it is older than time. It is "the mystery which hath been hidden from ages and from generations, but now is made manifest . . . which is Christ *in you*, the hope of glory" (Col. 1:26–27).

In one of the oldest temples in Japan there is a holy shrine composed of three inner shrines, or chambers. The temple of man's being also has three shrines.

In the outer court of the Japanese shrine there is a golden and bronze Buddha seated on the sacred lotus. In man's "temple not made with hands" there is the outer physical body that, like bronze, seems heavy, yet which in reality is gold because it is God. The many-handed goddess—the giver of all good gifts—is there too.

In the next inner shrine is the crystal Buddha, shining like the light of man's mind, the releaser of all darkness and representative of the transparent Presence in us all.

Then, stepping through a circular doorway, we enter the innermost shrine. Suddenly we realize that we are looking at a reflection of ourselves, for this innermost shrine is naught but a beautiful mirror.

We are so much greater than we think, even the least of us. We must establish ourselves in consciousness, for we will always be that which we ourselves establish. The most wonderful thing about Jesus was not the miracles and healings that He did, but the fact that He believed He was *worthy* to do them and that He knew He *was able* to do them.

No matter what makes up our lives, yours and mine, your life has *you* behind it, and my life has *me* behind it. Jesus did not come to save us from evil and deceit. He came to save us from ourselves and from the ignorance of not knowing.

We fall into the idea that once we come into a realization of God, there will be no more troubles or challenges. This is not true. The pattern of man's life is woven with experiences, and with experience may come frustration, disappointment, hurt, setbacks, humiliation, and many dark moments in which man is troubled. But nothing comes to us except the Father sends it, and nothing comes to us except we are ready to meet it. Our world is full of pressures but *we are full of God*.

EQUALIZE THE PRESSURES

One of the most widely recognized problems of this day is mental depression. Millions of people are mentally depressed and unable to cope with the simplest things in life. This depression is caused by outer pressures that press in upon man's mind, soul, and physical being. These pressures are externalized in man's body as physical exhaustion, aches, illness, and pain.

These pressures are in the invisible; they are so subtle that many times we cannot recognize or define them, yet they can have a devastating effect on our lives. We interpret these pressures as fear of loss, fear for loved ones, fear about money or world conditions, fear of another person's power over us.

Such pressures are not there because we are bad, nor are they there because we are good; rather, it is like the smog caused by man's ignorance and misunderstanding of natural laws. Pressure is the result of man trying to force his good into being by sheer strength of will. This forcing of life is unnatural and has a disintegrating effect. We can and we must counteract these pressures with a greater power. Scripture says, "Resist not evil but overcome evil with good" (Matt. 5:39). We must raise the pressure of our faith in our own inner invisible power to equalize the pressures from the outside world. We must fill our soul with so much strength, love, peace, and good will that we keep the balance of power within ourselves.

We must so establish ourselves in the belief in the unfolding pattern of life as good that no experience, situation, or condition of any kind can depress us, or press in upon us, or even impress us any more. Keep the God-pressure within—faith, love, and strength—high and be free from any outer pressure.

The pattern of man's life is made up of experiences, experiences that bring great joy or sorrow, disappointment, frustration, unhappiness. We sometimes go through one of these experiences feeling it is the end of everything; our heart is broken and our world shattered; but they are all life's way of making us great.

We sometimes feel that our humiliation is complete, our failure more than we can bear, and that we cannot go on.

We often say very foolish things during these moments, such as, "I cannot believe in God because if there is a God, why does this happen?" We say that we will never be "the same." This is so, because the truth of the matter is that we will be *greater and better*. We always believe in God because we always believe in good—somewhere, somehow.

LET GO OF THE PAST

From every experience we come up new beings, for we have let go of some old fear or worn-out opinion, prejudice, or belief. We must be free from old states of consciousness that are no longer adequate for our new and changing state of being. This is true of nations as well as of individuals. We must let go of the past for "God requireth that which is past" (Ecc. 3:15).

There is in reality no past with God, for such a state is in man's mind and must be surrendered to Truth. Before you can go on to the fullness of spirit and before you can eat at the feast of God—all good—you must let go of the past. The past lets go of you so you must let go of it.

Several years after the war, my son returned to Holland to visit the area in which he had landed as a paratrooper. He went back to visit the battlefield that he had known through that experience. All he could see were fields of tulips. The scar was healed. The past was gone forever. It was tulip time in Holland and every nook and cranny were filled with new and vibrant life for God erases all evidence. God heals the hearts and minds of men even more swiftly than He does nature because *at the center of every human being is the untouchable, inviolate Presence of God.*

In the Old and the New Testaments, this untouchable Presence is called "the Son of God." Every man, regardless of race, color, creed, or education has within him this Holy

Part. This is the *Untouchable You* that can never be humiliated, insulted, degraded, robbed, or hurt in any way by anything in all creation for it is unprofaned.

No matter what we have been taught or think about ourselves, we are created of God, and God is all—the one presence, power, and substance in all the world. This is the oldest truth in the universe, woven like a golden thread through every religion since antiquity.

IN THE IMAGE OF GOD

Since God is all and in all, what could we ourselves possibly be but God? Scientists have proved that there is only one primal substance, whether we call it First Cause, Energy, or God. Everything is related to and contained in this substance. We are all created "in the image," for we are all one. When we begin to recognize our oneness and let go of our separateness, we will bring down the mental prison walls that shut us off from God, from our good, and from each other.

Man was not only created in the image of God, with this image of God within, but is in the process of bringing forth the likeness of the image. As we live life and go through experiences, we are in the process of unfolding this image. In the process of developing, we find that nothing is wrong with us any more than there is something wrong with the little child who is not yet a man or woman, or with the plant that has not yet brought forth its blossoms. We are all somewhere in the process of unfoldment.

FORGETFULNESS OF GOD

Experiences come to us, and we are meant to live and move through them. We are not supposed to stay in one and continue to live and relive it. If we insist on reliving an experience after it has passed, it becomes like quicksand, and with each lingering moment it is more difficult to remove ourselves. We can try to remember hurt feelings, failure, unhappiness, and humiliation but they will slip away from us, for God has a wonderful way of letting his forgetfulness flow through the mind of man. Do not linger long with dead memories, hurt feelings, sorrow, resentment, and belief in failure. Let us set ourselves free from the results of these things in our lives.

If we would refuse to remember all the things that make us sad and empty, we would clear ourselves of much debris that blocks the flow of our good. We hear much about memory courses, but maybe a good course in forgetting might be a very helpful aid to our peace and joy. True action of life is forgetfulness. It is a healing balm that fills our minds and releases us from the burden of the past.

Let us know that as we forget we begin to live again. Let us not be afraid of "endings," for there is no end to anything. All endings are commencements; beyond every night there is always daybreak. All experiences are to be *walked through*. The Psalmist says, "Though I *walk through* the valley of the shadow of death, I will fear no evil . . . I will dwell in the house of the Lord forever."

Whatever we think is the end of something in our life is only the beginning of something else. Our minds turn to thoughts of those who have stepped into the Invisible, but just remember that if they could speak to us, they might use the words of the unknown poet who said, "When you have come where I have stepped, you will wonder why you wept." There is always progress.

There is always growth and unfoldment no matter at which end of life we stand. There are many verses in the Bible that need to be read with understanding. Many that have struck terror in our hearts have in truth a wonderful meaning. "Vengeance is mine; I will repay" is one example. This is true, for God does repay—in forgetfulness and in new love and life. In Second Corinthians it says, "My grace is sufficient for thee" (12:9). The love of God is sufficient to take care of every need under every circumstance. There is an inward healing that wipes away the memory of all unhappiness.

I knew a woman who, as a prisoner in a concentration camp during World War II, endured great suffering, humiliation, and unspeakable things. She said, "I have found in the years since the war, as I make my tea and do the everyday things of life, that it is as though these things never happened to me. I have found an untouchable part of me, deep within my innermost being, that is immaculate, pure, without stain or blemish, that has not been touched by any experience. Only the hate and the hurt we insist on remembering can touch us." All else is wiped out by the forgetfulness of God.

As nations, we need to find this untouchable Presence and forget the hates and hurts that have been in us all. Not a thing can touch the true spirit of man. If the experiences we have gone through collectively as nations can help us to let go of narrow beliefs, schisms caused by opinions, prejudices and differences, then we shall come forth worthy of the word brotherhood, and will find a better world.

As people and as nations, we have known the dishonesty, the cunning, and the craftiness brought forth through the mismanagement of our human powers, and we have witnessed the resultant losses. But even this cannot touch the Spirit within. In the innermost part of us, nothing can be lost and nothing stolen.

THE UNTOUCHABLE PART OF YOURSELF

We question why things happen, especially after we have done much for another person. Perhaps we have no right to do so much, if by so doing we discount the power of that other soul to do for itself. Everyone has the right to look to the Power within himself; he does not need to look to another human being. Every person must complete his own soul. We must let go and trust the Presence within; then nothing will be lost.

We go through many challenges that are like a refiner's fire, but in reality we cannot be touched even though we cry out and in every way seem affected. We may give up in despair, dishonor, and disgrace, yet there is still that part of us that has never been touched. Scripture tells us we can walk through the fire, and not be burned. Let us join the men in the story of old who experienced the fiery furnace and said, "Our God is able" (Dan. 3:17).

Is your God, your belief in good, able to take you through every experience? Yes, God is *able* but this Power must have you, for you are the expression or instrument of the invisible. There must be a oneness and a cooperation between man and his inner self. Man must find and touch this Untouchable Self within his own being. Only you can touch the God-presence within you. Nothing outside you can touch it.

We cannot *know* something that is not true. We cannot *know* that two times two equals five, because it is not true, but we can *believe* something that is not true. Therefore, that which is in the "outer" and is not true cannot touch the inner, real part of us.

There have been many misconceptions on the part of man even though he is the expression of God, with a spiritual heritage, great mental powers, and a body fearfully and wonderfully made. *He* has a world of plenty, of wealth untold, and yet man brings forth many contradictions in his life. The difficulty is that man does not know the untouchable part of himself.

Man has ignored himself, his true being. He has believed that he is an outer being with an outer field of activity, but the secret is out: Man's outer life is only a surface marker of the deep inner working of God. God, the indwelling spirit of man, functions through the process of thinking and feeling. Therefore, *man's thinking becomes a most important factor of his being—along with his ability not to think*.

THE VALUE OF NOT THINKING

Important as it is for man to think it is equally important for him to quiet his mind that he may receive through this same instrument—his mind—the directions, instructions, and pattern he is to follow. For man, *not to think* is important. Scripture says, "In such an hour as ye think not, the Son of man cometh" (Matt. 24:44). Man must cease the constant rampaging of his inquiring mind and learn to rest in the knowledge that God sustains him. When man accepts his good "without a doubt in his heart," then the good comes forth to fill his body and life.

Man's conscious thinking is to bring forth in the "outer" the material good that God has ordained for man, but *not thinking* brings forth the invisible good—the peace, love, joy, and good feeling that are man's divine birthright. In *not thinking*, we make of our mind an open door to all good. Then our minds, bodies, and lives are filled with the true expression of life.

Man is changing rapidly from his present outer expression of a successful, fast-talking, scheming being to a new being as different from the old as is the butterfly from the

Chrysalis =

cocoon. Man is already both the old and the new, for he is in the chrysalis stage of the new man. A great deal now depends upon his guidance, direction, and action from within.

Man goes forward with great gusto in the "outer" until he gets to a stalemate in his own being where he cannot explain his dilemma to himself. He cannot understand why he has so much and yet so little.

Man feels empty and this emptiness causes many excesses in his life. When man is empty, he drinks, eats, and rushes about trying subconsciously to fill this emptiness, but all he truly needs is to find God within himself. The reason for his frustration is that *he does not go on* to his greater unfoldment; he will never be satisfied until he becomes what he was created to be. His greater unfoldment is from within. It is spiritual, for it is caused by the activity of Spirit within him.

Man feels the unfolding pattern and has moved into his new life and field of activity in the "outer," but he has not followed this up with equal activity in the inner. Man is working with the invisible in electronics, electricity, and atomic power, but he has not made his *conscious* contact with the invisible All-Power in his personal being. He already calls the power he must find for himself by many names, yet the true name of this All-Power is God.

Man cannot go further into his new advancement. The door to complete revelation and use of the invisible in his life is closed until he accepts the knowledge that is now his and acts upon it. The new chapter in human history is opening. The old human nature is being left behind us. The limited, fearful, selfish, or striving man is on his way out. This man is obsolete. A new man, based on radiation that pours out of his heart, must come forth out of man's old cocoon.

THE TWO THINGS MAN MUST DO

This new man *must know* and use all the inner powers of his being because he *must be aware* of his true self—God within. He *must create* harmony, peace, love, health, and freedom in his immediate surroundings. These two things every soul *can* do right now to set free the new man within. First, each must establish in his own conscious mind that God is within him. He must know that a Power lives and moves and has its being in him. This Power is the movement of life in man's body and mind.

Man knows that there is something greater within him than he has yet brought forth. Man must claim and acknowledge this Power within that is unfolding through him the greater good he is destined to have and to be. Man must, in thought and word, keep his attention focused on this inner Presence until the truth of its being in him becomes as sure to him as that of the simple statement "Two times two equals four." The second thing man must do is to *set free* and *establish* peace, power, love, and good feeling right where he is. He must prove to himself that *he can establish his own* sense of well-being and right relationships with his world, whether it be in his home, business, work, with the people closest to him, or with whomever he has a contact of any kind. There is a much greater power for man, but he must be true to the "little" things if he is to be trusted with the "greater." When he does these two things, then he is ready to receive greater power.

In order to know his *Inner Power*—"God"—he must *use* the powers he has. If he talks about faith, he must have faith, believing when he cannot see. He must believe in the Invisible. He must stand in faith.

He must use his power of love *to love*. He must not just

talk about love. He must be a radiant center of love wherever he is. He must build his life on this power.

He must use strength, not talk about it as a theory. To use strength is to *stand* before the outer picture of sickness, fear, lack, or whatever it may be, and *know* that there is something greater.

Man must know that he has the power within him to bring everything in his life to a satisfying conclusion. He must know that he is a law unto himself, for every man is God in his living, physical expression.

Spiritual Qi Gong — goal

1) Claim Oneness with the
   — Focus on inner presence
    of God Force

2) Establish Vibration energy
   Peace, Power
   Love, Joyfulness

3) Believe in the Invisible

4) Believe in Frater

5) Power of Love

6) Radiant Love

7) Use Strength / knowing
   in the face of Fear & Lack

6. Am I My Brother's Keeper?

The greatest challenge of our life is our relationship with other human beings. By this, I mean *all* other human beings, including every living soul, from our loved ones to the ones who live in the farthest corner of the universe.

All relationships are truly rooted in mind and feeling, not based upon physical proximity or propinquity. Because this is true, mental and emotional disturbances have the power to rob us of health, peace of mind, wealth, and even our sense of well-being. Since mental and emotional disturbances are within *us*, it is *we* who are affected by them.

We can have mental relationships with people we have never seen except in the news of the day, and because of our reactions to them even these seemingly insignificant associations affect us.

The question of Cain, "Am I my brother's keeper?" echoes down through the ages and rings in our ears. We too ask the same question, "Am I my brother's keeper?" The answer is, "Yes and no."

WHEN THE ANSWER IS NO

No, you are not your brother's keeper if you define keeper as "one who watches, guards, or takes care of another." *No*, if you think you have anything to do with his choice of what he should or should not do. *No*, if you think that you should direct the life of another. You should never give anyone advice or try to manipulate him into decisions or actions. Never. His guidance must come from within.

In our complicated civilization, we often need and seek advice on law or principle, but here we are referring to outer personal decisions. The decisions and choices that arise from the innermost parts of our heart and being are those for which we need *no* advice.

The children under our care and guidance are an entirely different matter. Human beings who have reached the age of decision should make their own decisions *in every instance*. Otherwise, we become a stumbling block or a crutch in their lives. Children, however, are given to us to be loved and sustained with our consciousness until they can establish one of their own. Even so, we are not to prolong the time of guidance beyond a reasonable time of unfoldment. Sometimes we find ourselves trying to guide and influence a person who has been of the age of decision for twenty or thirty years.

We can often persuade another to act against his own inner guidance by our approval or disapproval, expressed in just a word or even by a look. We should leave every soul completely to his own God-direction. To your own inner self be true, and allow everyone else to be true to his own inner God-guidance. If one must think of another person and how that person is going to react before he himself can follow the God-direction in his own heart, then he does not have freedom in the action of his own spirit.

The first commandment is, "Thou shalt have no other gods before me." You must not allow another to come between you and your God-self, and, in turn, you must not permit yourself to exercise such an influence over another. If before a person can make a decision in his own soul he must think of you, then *you* are out of place.

God's purpose must not be thwarted in a human being, for when it is we find tension, sickness, lack, frustration, and inner failure. The soul of man must be free to unfold; it must not be held back by the approval or disapproval of anyone.

WHEN THE ANSWER IS YES

Yes, you are your brother's keeper in that, *in your own mind*, you are to keep every man in his perfect relationship with God. *Yes*, you are your brother's keeper if you help him to keep his own God-path, which is his own inner-direction and inner-knowing and guidance.

Yes, you are your brother's keeper if you sustain him as he moves out into his greatest and most perfect expression, and if you give him the freedom to do what his own inner spirit desires him to do. Always refer another human being to his own inner feelings. Each has his own built-in receiving set, and if he does not get his directions immediately, let him wait. Waiting is also growth and unfoldment and a part of the pattern of life. "Life is movement and rest," says Jesus, in the Gospel of Thomas. We think things are dormant when they are still in the process of forming within.

If people come to you for personal direction or advice, do not give it to them. Rather, turn them back within their own being. You may not be able to say to them, "What does God say?" but you can say, "What does your heart say?" or "How do *you* think and feel about it?"

God does great work within the seed while it seems to be waiting. Every man should wait upon the action and decision of his own heart. We should all wait upon the law, the still small voice, of our own being. We are making the greatest strides forward when we make progress *within* ourselves.

We are in this world to express and fulfill our own faith, love, and understanding. We are to image, to will, to do, and to be as we move forward to unfold our own inner God-pattern. The God-presence within is always moving through you, unfolding you toward freedom, success, and happiness. But remember, every other living being has come for the same reason—to unfold from within his own being.

God gave the same power to all. It is not *yours* exclusively. You have not come to order, direct, and take care of everyone else. Your God-voice is for you and *you alone*, for every person has his own private line.

This does not mean that opposition and differences of opinion are not good, for in truth they are both healthy and natural. Such opposition makes our own position strong, as a heavy clod of earth makes a plant strong as it pushes through.

If you are called upon to make a stand, make it from *within* and it will be right and true for you. Have conviction in your beliefs at any particular time. You may change your mind later, but for the time being stand for what you believe and think.

Allow every person to make his own stand, although it may be opposed to your deepest conviction. Martin Luther stood and was convinced of what he believed when he said, "Here I stand, so help me God." Have courage wherever you find yourself. Stand still, be not afraid of results in the "outer," be untouched by the opinions or judgments of others whether they be friends, loved ones, or even foes. Learn to receive your guidance and move with it on all occasions. Remember, it is for you and you alone. It was not given to you to maneuver, manipulate, and work upon other people.

FIND YOUR OWN WAY

Each man's way is right and good for him. There are as many ways of reaching the kingdom of good as there are people to travel, and to each his own way. Jesus said, "I am the way" (John 14:6), and you can say, "I am the way for *me*," but remember it is *your* way, not the *only* way.

We all dislike dictatorship, yet in our everyday life, in families, clubs, businesses, homes, there is a fine dividing line between dictatorship and freedom. Do not dictate or be dictated to, but pray and listen for your own guidance.

All association with others is in our mind and our feelings. All relationships are within us. *You are your relationship* with all that is in your world. You may think there are those out there doing this and that, slighting you, disliking you, hindering you, or loving you, but let us understand that all these things are in us. If you are lonely and unhappy, the whole world seems cold and thoughtless. If you are always finding fault with yourself, the world seems hard and cynical and people seem to be always taking advantage of you.

If you are filled with love, the whole world is lovely, beautiful, and every day is filled with wonder and joy. If you are happy, everything seems easy and you have patience with people; it is because things are right with you and in you.

Your relationship with your inner God-self is reflected in every cell of your body and every corner of your life. When you withdraw and feel empty and incomplete, everyone forgets you and you are left out. There is nothing wrong with your world. There is nothing wrong with you. You just do not relate yourself to the image and expression of your own consciousness.

WE NEED EACH OTHER

The greatest gift that has been given us is other human beings. They are our teachers, our pupils, the ones who foil and frustrate us; yet there is a mighty symphony being played in every encounter. We are never quite aware of the force and scope of the invisible counterchange that is constantly taking place between human beings. This exchange is food for our souls, and we cannot live a balanced, complete life without it. Loneliness is not the actual absence of human beings but of the invisible essence of life that we share with one another.

Our very being is influenced and molded by others; not just by those who are near and dear to us but also by the casual touch of the spirit of a passerby. It is Spirit moving upon Spirit. Often a person who makes a fleeting contact with us can change the pattern and trend of our life while a close friend may make only a lukewarm impression.

It is our failure if we do not grow strong by the opposition of others. It is sad to be a vassal when one was created to be king. We are together in order to grow individually. We are not placed in the human environment to force others to think as we do or act as we might. Nor are we here to strive to be like them. We are here to be ourselves—our true God-selves stemming from a pattern within us as sure as the pattern of the butterfly or the rose. We were created and born free; we take on our human bondage.

MAKE NO SMALL PLANS

We are together that we may all develop "in wisdom and stature and in favour with God and man" (Luke 2:52). There is a certain boldness required to accomplish life. Nearly every unfrustrated soul lives with unhesitating boldness. We shall live and like life if we are bold in our living. If you are not bold, you can be overwhelmed by the outer witnesses of life. The outer witnesses are other people and their differences and personalities. All who give to humanity do so because of outstanding boldness. Boldness is a necessity when you stand with God. By bold, I do not mean brash or overbearing, but rather the definition that Webster gives as obsolete, which is *confidant, wholly assured*.

We must be bold enough to commit ourselves to a position in life and to be unafraid to change that position with the arrival of greater understanding. We are not to be lukewarm. The lukewarm man hovers around waiting for an indication of how things are going to be. Such a person is not a leader, not even of himself. We must each be bold enough to take our life in our hands. It takes boldness to move when you cannot see the way. It takes boldness to stand with your heart and mind against another to whom you owe allegiance. Your first allegiance is to your self. "Be true to ME," and know that "ME" is your inmost self.

The words "bold," "boldly," "boldness" appear many times in the Scriptures. I cannot find the word "moderation" once. The rewards of moderation are modest rewards, likely to accomplish nothing for you. Be bold enough to move toward your heart's desire. Your heart's desire is the still, small voice of God unfolding your pattern within you. Let us make no small plans, for God is great and so are we.

THE TRANSPARENT RACE

We are divided into races, types, nations, and families. There are differences in the color of the skin, in the shape of the head, in the height and the frame. Some men have said that some races are superior to others. These men who speak of superior races probably belong to the race they call "superior," because the great Power that is in us makes us all feel superior. God within makes each man feel his importance and this is good. But we must remember God dwells in all. Here, in this knowing, we *are* our brother's keeper. We are wise if we keep him there.

Every man belongs to the superior race. In the sight of God every man is created equal, but each man is in a different state of unfoldment. No man is more superior spiritually than another, but some men are more adept at expressing their indwelling spirit than others. All men haven't found out about their true creation but have accepted the belief of man that speaks of superiority—not knowing that he who speaks is thinking of the outer superiority of the world of things.

Any man can develop his spiritual counterpart at any time. Each man and woman must remember that the wisdom of man is foolishness to God. Each human being must awaken to the knowledge that he or she belongs to the Transparent Race, a race of spiritual beings. It doesn't matter about the outer differences, for all belong to the Transparent Race. They may be red or black or yellow or so-called white; but we are all, even now, Spiritual Man. The invisible Spirit is the real of all. Spirit is transparent. God is transparent and lives and dwells in all creation. Let us be too wise to classify any man or woman except in their highest good. To be transformed is to be aware of our true self.

Every human being has the mouth of God in his innermost part. I learned this lesson in the war years. One of my sons was a paratrooper, and on D day he jumped in the European theater of war. I was very fearful and I sought out a wise friend to allay my fears. Let me tell you what I learned that day. This was my message: "Your son has his own indwelling Presence that guides and directs him—as do we all. His own still small voice will tell him exactly what to do when he jumps from the plane and touches the ground. It will say to him, 'Lie down—wait—now you can run to that tree—now to the building.' He will listen breathlessly and will be obedient to it. That is the voice of God directing and guiding him. Don't send any fear static to be picked up by his receiving set—let him be free to listen to the only safe guide." Let us learn to free our brother and our loved ones, and every man. Do not send them messages of weakness, failure, and unhappiness. Love all so much that you place them in the care and keeping of the Almighty God.

Sometimes we have a feeling that others have failed us, misused us, and we have no faith and trust in anyone. Did it ever occur to you that they are a part of the infinite plan of God for you, that only through what they do will you be forced to do what you must do? Joseph of long ago had brothers who took him from his father and sold him into slavery—only that he might go to Egypt and fulfill his destiny, and later be able to say to his brothers, "Ye thought evil against me, but God meant it unto good" (Gen. 50:20). Perhaps when Jesus called Judas "friend" (Matt. 26:50), he knew that he too was a part of the infinite plan.

All of life is change and growth. Love, forgiveness, and mellowness are a part of growth. If you have held something against someone for years and years, know that they have grown and changed and so have you. We must drop forever the shackles that hold us back.

The time is right for the advent of a new man. This man comes forth by constant experiences and exchanges of human beings. Experiences are like pruning shears as well as loving hands that press the earth close so that the plant may bring forth much fruit. Experiences and relationships with fellow humans, their comings and their goings, are part of the infinite plan of life. Did not one of the greatest teachers say, "It is expedient for you that I go away, for if I go not away, the Comforter will not come to you" (John 16:7). For the new man to come forth does not mean that the old man is destroyed. He is "transformed by the renewing of his mind" (Rom. 12:2).

7. Choice Is Our Privilege

The door is open, the feast is laid, the way is unrestricted, the time is *now*. The invitations are out; all are invited, every human being is included. The writing is clear and it is not upon the wall but in the hearts of men, for all are chosen. Strange as it may seem, all are ready.

Not all are aware and many would deny that they are going, because the finished realm is hidden just out of view and is reached by an inner, little-used door. Nevertheless, all is prepared. Nothing is left undone and no power on earth can stay the fulfillment of the plan. The purpose is finished and *we are the strangers at the door*. Strangers, only because we have not come all the way and this entrance is strange to us, yet it and all that lies beyond is ours and has always been ours.

We hesitate, wait, and turn back undecided and uncertain. We falter and we long to go forward at the same time. Something very strange and wonderful is happening to us.

We are drawn by an irresistible force, by a power that is gentle and unhurried; yet it is not only the greatest power on earth but the *only* power on earth and in heaven. We are in a unique position, for we must go but we must move under our own volition. It must be of our own free will and we must work in perfect freedom. The choice is completely ours.

No other living soul can deter us or hurry us, and no power on earth can stand between us and our destination. Even we cannot interfere for long, for it has not been given to us to fail in this field of action. It is an open invitation that sooner or later must be answered, and it will be answered by all.

What does this all mean? It means that mankind is ready for tremendous changes. All human beings are right now in the midst of these changes. They are deep inner changes that are already affecting our outer life. Man is and has been making contact with an inner source that is changing his world. Old states of mind and ways of action are dropping away.

Soon man will be unable to do anything without conscious awareness and effort to work with this power that directs him from within. He will not move or be moved by any power except an inner invisible movement in his own heart and mind. This power is God.

The power that moves man always has been God and always will be God. The only difference now is that *every man shall know that every movement and activity in him is God.* The great Spirit of God is going to have its way in us, whether we agree or not.

We are *all*—and I mean every living human being, regardless of race, color, or creed—going to be drawn into the magic spiritual awakening and an outer awareness. Where there has been division, there will be unity of purpose. Man will work with mind and heart, not just with mind alone.

The great Spirit of God is putting simple little people in high places to confound the wise. He is using those who are open and receptive in high and low places, wherever He finds them. He is using shocking and breathtaking experiences and calamities to shake man out of his stupor and lethargy.

FREEDOM UNDER GOD

Every man has freedom under God and there is no freedom for man without God. Man will only be free as he is aware of this invisible power we call "God." Freedom is a state of being; it is the result of a consciousness of complete oneness and the resultant release that follows this state of mind.

As we wander, grow, and unfold, we are unaware of our true heritage and what it entails, much as a little child at play is unaware of the adult self that it is to be. So long as we are unaware that we are cared for—unaware that the creator of the universe is *our mind and breath and life,* and that a mighty pattern is unfolding in and through us—we will be troubled and insecure.

Until we know—not *believe,* but *know*—that we only have to lend ourselves, surrender ourselves, give our mind (which is thinking) and our heart (which is feeling), and our full outer attention to the invisible Power that moves our breath, body, thoughts, and actions—until we know this truth about ourselves and others we will not have freedom, and every move will be hampered. We must step out in our life on our *knowing.*

So long as we feel that we are divided from God or are aware of other people and situations, as either against us or detrimental to us, we have let go of our freedom. We complicate our lives. We think that we are on our own. We begin by thinking that we will go our way and others can go theirs.

This is a sad state of mind. We should never feel or think

that we are on our own. When we feel that we are on our own, we begin to look after ourselves, take care of "our" interests, cope with situations and conditions, and then we have walked out on God, our good.

The loneliest soul on earth is the soul that feels it is on its own with just the outer material self. The happiest and most complete being on earth is the one who is aware of the inward pull, who feels the inner strength and power, who relies upon this inner knowing, turning to it unhesitatingly, trusting it completely, and seeking for it in all others.

One who is strong in an inward relationship with himself, his fellow man, his world, and therefore his God, is the fortunate man of today.

Any man whose eyes, mind, plans, and feelings are focused on the "outer," looking to the outer for gain and guidance, will find no freedom but will become more and more confused, more and more disturbed.

In the past, the ordinary man has lived unaware of his own greatness, unaware that when he was given life and breath, he was also, at that instant, given a continuing and sustaining power. This power continues in him to this moment, either with his conscious awareness or unheeded and unrecognized.

Man is maturing and he must awaken to his potential power, as youth becomes aware of adulthood. This finished realm in the inner part of man is a living, tangible aliveness, a freedom beyond any concept that man has yet evolved.

The time is at hand for man to come of age spiritually, to know the truth about himself, and to live in this awareness. He is not just to believe he can someday come into the fullness of life; he is to know that he is in that fullness—that *he is there now.*

SAFETY IN UNION

The revelation of this age is the fatherhood of God and the brotherhood of man. Every man is to know that the die is cast; the handwriting is on the heart of man and none shall be exempt. Old religions are wavering. Changes are being made in the "outer" which reveal to us the trend in the inner. We are all being gathered in. Every man in religion and state is feeling a pull to understand and belong to every other man. We are eager to belong, to be unified, because our soul tells us that our only safety is in union.

We are becoming aware that every human being is God, expressing; and that each is important to the balance of all. Freedom under God comes when we have no hate or resentment against any man; when we can look at every man and know that his actions are his unfoldment, his interpretation or consideration of that which is within him.

We shall no longer say, "What he is doing can harm me," for we shall know that nothing on earth or in heaven above can harm us when we know that we are established in God. Nothing—no person or persons or their action or lack of action, no group of people, no visible or invisible power—can be against us. Nothing can touch us when we know that we are established in the truth of life.

The truth is that we are not just outer physical beings, cut off, prey of time and tide; we are created under a divine law that forever works in harmony and order. This is a law that is as orderly as the seasons and the stars. This law is working even when we are crying out, fearful and denying any help or cause.

We grope in the "outer" for help but, one by one, every outer support deserts us until we are driven back. We are driven back into our own hearts to find that here within us, having been here all the time, is the strength and vitality that sustains life and all conditions.

What another man thinks or feels or believes cannot affect us unless we move into his consciousness. Unless there is something in our consciousness to attract a situation, no experience on earth can touch us. Like Jesus, there must be "nothing in me" (John 14:30) to meet the untrue. When we are established in God—our unseen true good of mind and soul—nothing can touch us.

I know this could be a point of argument, for our minds could cite many instances where there has been injustice, plunder, robbery of the innocent, but Webster says that the innocent are naïve, untaught. This is not knowing. Not knowing that out of every human happening, good comes. We must know our relationship to God. Our relationship to God is a oneness or *sameness*, we are the same as God. "There are diversities of operations but it is the same God which worketh all in all" (I Cor. 12:6). We are God, pressed into outer form, but we are identical in essence and have a function which is visible life. There is no freedom without this knowledge. Otherwise, we are torn by the seeming reality of the "outer," without the wisdom to know that it is a passing panorama. The *real* of us is unchangeable. There is no freedom or security without God-knowledge.

People who live without God, without a consciousness of good, who are filled with resentment toward others, constantly finding fault, nourishing grievances and hate because of their own insecurity, change the very chemistry of their bodies. In fact, if a person's mind is constantly filled with fear, hate, hurt feelings, and unhappiness, a psychopathic reaction affects them and they are not normal; they cannot dwell in freedom. Freedom under God is the power to dwell with one's fellow man in peace and understanding.

OUR DIVINE PLACE IN THE UNIVERSE

Our education should not teach us of our shortcomings and other men's greatness; it should teach each one his own divine place in the universe. We are here for a great and wonderful purpose and this purpose is our relationship with other people. The greatest power for man's growth and unfoldment is another human being; yet differences are the divine law of life.

Our divine place in the universe is a place of balance serving the invisible and adjusting to the visible. It empowers us to believe in the power of Spirit in the midst of humanity; to know that as sons of God we eat and sleep in human form, and by our knowing enjoy our double life, for we are both human and divine.

Spirit does not fail man and life does not overcome him. Wherever we find hate and insecurity, we find fear; we fear those who do not think and act the same as we do. We are so insecure that we have to protect our own opinions because we are without the basic truth of all truths.

You shall know the truth of yourself and your *truth* shall make *you* free. God dwells in every man, and man's freedom is in this inner wisdom and knowledge of his true self.

The great invitation of life is to *know*. The reason we are not aware of the high calling and purpose of life is because we feel lost; yet we cannot be lost, for we are made of the essence of God and Scripture says that not even a sparrow falls to the ground without the Father.

TO HOLD IS TO LOSE

Loss is a fearful word to man because his greatest fear is loss. He is afraid he will lose his position in life; his opportunity, money, or influence; he is afraid he will lose his power, his loved ones, or his life. So he is haunted by the idea of loss.

In one sense, "loss" means ruin, destruction, but it also has another meaning: Webster tells us that "loss" is the "act or fact of failing to win, gain, obtain, or utilize." So, if we feel lost or in a state of loss, we have failed to win something or gain certain things or obtain something; we have not used or utilized what we have. Because we have not used it, it seems lost to us; but that which is real cannot be lost. It will always be there. We seem to lose many things in life. We lost our babyhood, our childhood, our schooldays, but nothing has really been "lost," for we have used, utilized, and obtained something all along the way.

Sometimes it seems that we get lost in a small corner of life, as though we were to get lost in a closet of our house and be unable to realize that the whole house is there, just beyond the door. We get lost in some little portion or part of life, sometimes in hurt feelings, in some human relationship, or in our bodies or business.

Life is onward and upward. Everything is being translated into something higher, and we must not get lost in a small part. We must realize the greater power and life. We may lose sight of our goal for a moment but we can utilize, use, gain, and win again the realization of the great moving panorama of life. Our soul is never bound by any person, situation, or condition. Our soul is never tied to any particular time or expression. The soul marches on. Regardless of our seeming stupidity, our handicaps, nothing can hold back the progress of that innermost part of us. It cannot be held by any experience. Nothing that has ever happened can defeat the soul.

Your soul has wings and it leaves all that is low, sordid, petty, and unhappy. It leaves all defeat and disgrace. It also leaves fame, fortune, and acclaim, for the soul of man does not tarry.

We try to tie our soul to some unhappy experience, some failure or mistake, but it rebels. Nor can we hold it to some happy, breathtaking experience, some beautiful love or unforgettable moment in life, for it will not linger for long, but hurries on. We must let it go on to every new experience, for every day of life is a day of experience.

Do you know where true loss comes? True loss, the kind that robs and weakens man, is holding on to the moment after the moment is gone. This is the only loss in the world, because when you hold on to a moment, you lose the next one. No matter how sweet a moment may be, let it go. If you try to hold on to it, it becomes bitter. It is only the new moment that brings new sweetness.

Whether the moment is sweet or humiliating or filled with shame, you must always go on. If we stop to reconsider, to judge ourselves, to judge others, we have true deprivation. We can receive a blessing from every moment by letting the moment go. We possess just for the moment. Life is accepting, possessing, and letting go. The coming is the joy of life. The experiencing is the crown of life; but holding to the experience is the loss.

We have many great moments in life. We could name them but let us take, for instance, graduation. Let us imagine you are valedictorian of your class, chosen to deliver the farewell message. You are letter-perfect, garbed in your graduation cap and gown, and you are at a high point. You get up; you speak. You are truly great. All acclaim you and you are filled with the thrill of well-being. Your speech is over, the well-wishers come by, the hall empties, and there you stand—that moment is gone. If you cannot let it go and take the next moment with equal joy and power, you suffer true loss.

There are people who have had experiences but have never moved past the incident or condition. Physically, they live, but never with their minds do they forget, let go, move on to new life.

Something else is waiting to happen, but it cannot happen for it is carried by the next moment and we will not go on to embrace it.

No matter how great a moment may be, let it go. Even in moments of failure and humiliation, remember to go on. It is just as important to move on from a moment of triumph as it is from a moment of failure.

We hold too tightly. Like the child who catches the butterfly in its hand, we crush the moment and we cannot go on. Man has thought that he is a creature of circumstances, but man is the creator of his own environment, and in this power to create lies his freedom and power. Until he knows this about himself and for himself, nothing will change.

ACTING ON FAITH

Do we really have choice? Yes, we do have choice. We have choice at every point in our life. Whether we take it or not is another matter.

So many times life seems hopeless, difficulties seem endless, problems seem overwhelming. In response, we do one of three things: set out to find an answer within our own self; give up to the situation and prepare ourselves to live with it; simply vegetate and do nothing. So you see that we have already made a choice.

We must make the choice in order to have the answer and to have the fulfillment; if we do this we automatically draw to us the power that completes it. When we act on faith that there is a way, even though we cannot see it, we draw to us the invisible essence and power that carries us through.

We choose what we will think and believe. No one else

can make that choice. We may have those who try to put into our mind discouragement and fear, but we are the keeper of the gate of the mind. The choice belongs to the individual.

Faith is always our invisible choice. Faith is guidance to finding that which satisfies our soul and makes us feel right. We can only live with ourselves when we feel right—don't forget that. Our choice must make us feel right. It must establish in us a sense of well-being.

We do not have much to give to life until we express our true selves and until we are functioning from the highest within us. We must learn to know our own true thoughts and to distinguish them from the crosscurrent of world thoughts and race beliefs. We must move into the great arena of life and do the things we were created to do.

We have the choice, but how do we know what to choose? Faith is the guide in choice; good feeling completes and seals the choice. What is our good? It is to feel good inside about a condition or situation; when something within says, "This is it." We must learn to trust this inner judgment. This is not the "thinking mind" with all its reasons, schemes, ways, and means. Rather, it is a still, small something that we feel, and we do not know why or how we feel it.

WHAT IS "PROPER"?

When we stand in a threadbare garment of fear and it causes us to tremble; when we are upset, beset on every side; if we are taking ourselves apart, condemning ourselves; if we are saying, "Why did I do this or that," we are separated and apart.

When we come to the place where we must give all our time to our troubles, when we are cluttered up with possessions, distracted by ambition, anxious about the future, filled with wants and worries that harass us on all sides, we are at this place for a special purpose. It is a time of choice.

What is choice? Webster says that to choose means "to think proper." But what is "proper"? Proper means "belonging to one," "one's own." Choice then means to take one's own. One's own can only be found in the innermost heart and feeling nature, it is that "something" within that urges us to our full expression, an inner movement that will not let us go, a movement we call desire or longing. This is our own. Desire means 'from Father.'

There is an answer, a solution that is our own, proper for us. When there is discord with others, angry words that upset us, or condemnation of ourselves or another, it is time to think proper, understanding of course that thinking is more than the outer movement of mind, but is a deep inner conviction and longing for true expression.

Let us not degrade ourselves or hurt another because of experiences. Know that our need is for the tempering of our souls in the fire of living and that this is where we make our greatest growth.

Find the right relationship to every experience. Do not look back to any experience and feel shame. From the word "shame" comes the word "sham," which means having something to do with nothing. Every instant of your life has been important, and right now is the most important of all. Do not be afraid of meeting what lies in your life. Do not be afraid of differences—differences of any kind—whether they have to do with people or opinions. All power has been given us. We may retreat or withdraw, but we will be strengthened because we have moved.

Never run away, for you have power to walk the path that is your own, and don't forget it. Make that choice, now. Do you make the choice or do you run away from experience? To run is choice too. To run is to choose to keep the fearful, hateful, unhappy thing, because during every moment you run it "sticketh closer than a brother."

We read of people giving their lives to this or for that. We don't like to think of people giving their lives and yet we give ours every day. Every day of living requires our life. This is where choice lies. To what are you giving your life?

Sometimes we find ourselves fleeing, avoiding the things that lie before us. Not to live the life we were given to live is bad choice. We find ourselves avoiding people and experiences. We duck around corners, we cross streets, but we are only failing to meet something in ourselves. We are running away from what we have to give.

Sometimes we run away from an impossible problem, one that seems to be insurmountable or unsolvable, but this is choice too. We choose not to face it. We say that we live here or there, but we really live in our mind and all choice is made *there*.

DON'T ASK WHY

Let us become aware of ourselves, for all that comes to us must be met and we have the power to meet it. Meeting life is wonderful and exciting. We can choose to have triumph and power or we can choose to worry, fret, hate, and cling to unhappiness. Sometimes we do not forgive ourselves for the past. We say, "Why did I do that?" Blessed is the man who is no longer under the bondage of the question "Why?" "Why" is many times the quicksand of regret.

We do not ask why the dog barks or why the cat meows and the owl hoots; nor do we ask why we breathe. We know that it is because these things are natural. They are an expression of life.

Our difficulty is that we are always trying to find the answer in our intellect. We will never find in our outer mind a true answer about the things that are in our heart. We may find the answer to how many miles it is to the next town or what day it is, but we will never find why people are the way they are or even why we are as we are. The answer will always be in the innermost part of us, in our heart, so that is where we must seek it, and when we find it we will know that it is our expression of life.

If we think we have made a wrong choice, if we carry a sense of guilt, fear, condemnation, we have made the choice to carry it—not that we need to.

We cannot harm another person. We might steal their money or their time, but we cannot rob them of spiritual or mental good. Only *they* can rob themselves of that. You may think that some action of yours of the past has harmed others, misled them, or changed the tide of their lives, but the choice was theirs; yours was the choice you made to believe this.

"Die daily" to whatever happens; be finished with it; let it go that your next good may come.

We regret so much and condemn so much that we carry untold and unnecessary burdens. All that happens to us is part of our schooling, our growth, our fulfillment and unfoldment. The past is nothing but the past. If we choose to live, we choose the greatest gift of all. Release. Let go.

You have the choice and only you have it for you. You alone can accept the invitation, the invitation that is open to us all, the invitation to peace and to power.

8. The Meaning of Prayer

Prayer is the missing link between God and man.

Prayer is the most accelerated mind-action known. Prayer takes the substance of God and forms a world and everything in this world. Prayer lifts a *man* to the fulfillment of God. Prayer, the greatest power on earth, is the action through which man releases his true self into the world through his body, heart, mind, and life.

Prayer is the daily acceptance and release of God-substance in and through each individual. God knows our need, but prayer is to establish ourselves in this need. It is our acceptance. The Power of God reacts immediately to prayer. You have the power to release the hidden energy of God.

Prayer is not just communion "with God"; it is the way in which man establishes the Divine Energy in its right relationship to every living thing. Prayer is the act of stepping into the perfect unfoldment of God in ourselves.

Prayer is contemplation, reverie, dreaming, waiting, relaxed knowing. Prayer is action, laughter, joy, achievement at work or play, for prayer is always a consciousness of the eternal good that is *ours*.

PRAYER IS ACCEPTANCE

Prayer is complete acceptance of the things "we have need of." Prayer establishes a state of consciousness whereby we can suspend the conscious fight for every need that is called the daily struggle. Through prayer we allow the invisible good to come forth, first in our mind and heart, then in our body, family, business, and life.

Prayer is elevating the mind to the *highest*. Take your mind to good if you want to see the power of good in action. Every thought or action that reaches out for something higher or better is prayer. Prayer is the spontaneous desire for a greater expression of any good on any level.

Talking to yourself about yourself and the good within and without is one of the most fruitful forms of prayer. You cannot ask for anything that has not already been given to you. Your desire for it is the thing itself, moving into your life. You pray to clear your vision that you may accept that which is seeking you. Prayer does not change what you are, but through prayer you are lifted to what you truly are. Pray for the ability to pray more completely.

Prayer is something *you* must do. Only you can do it *for you*. You pray to know the next step each day, to know what you should do, where you should go. You pray when you cannot see the way.

If you do not know how to pray, say "God! God! God!" A prayer without words often receives the swiftest, fastest answer.

We pray when we do not know what we want—when we only know that we want the *great release* that comes from *knowing* there is One who is responsible. *Yes*—responsible for you! Into the hands and plans of the Creator we surrender all needs, fears, doubts, and hurts.

In prayer we become as little children speaking to their father. The child knows that his father sustains him and takes care of his needs. A child is not afraid of its father.

Prayer is not a duty or a habit, but a pouring forth of your heart in gratitude for every breath, every moment of life, every experience, good or bad. It is enough to know that God is there, and while you cannot see your way, remember that it is clearly marked in the invisible realm of Spirit.

Prayer is not asking for things, not even the best things. Prayer is the lifting of the consciousness to the place where these things are. All things come through the mind of man, and to our mind we must go for the thing desired.

PRAYER IS PRAISE

When a man prays he gives praise and thanksgiving for the ever-present Power within him, which is, this moment and every moment, the life in his body and the mind he thinks with and the action of his feeling nature. God is that which is moving through *you*, *"being" you today*.

This Presence is *being* each one of us regardless of color, race, religion, or division of any kind. True prayer is praise of the One Power and Presence in every living thing. This is recognition of the *real* of everything.

Praise expands everything. People, plants, children, animals, even inanimate things, respond to praise. I cannot tell you how, but try it for yourself. If you want more of anything, praise and give thanks and you shall have it.

Try praise on your body, your family, your home, your business, your work, and your friends. The whole creation responds to praise. A weak body responds as vitality and strength. A fearful heart responds as peace and trust. Shattered nerves become poise and power.

Praise a failing business into prosperity and success, a wayward child into a balanced being. Praise want and insufficiency into supply and support. Praise is giving thanks for all things, not as they seem to be, but as they truly are in the plan of God.

THE WRONG PRAYER

Prayer is not telling your troubles to God; prayer is not supplication; this is to pray amiss. Prayer is not a multiplication of negative words—"I am nothing. I know nothing except that I am here, full of need, misery, ignorance, doubt, and fear." This is but a review of a soul shut off from God. This is not prayer.

Prayer is not shouting at God to tell Him of our troubles, difficulties, hurts, heartaches; this is only rearranging our own unhappy thoughts. True prayer is not begging or pleading for what is *already ours*. We accept all things with *our own* conscious recognition which is the power of mind that *unites us with it*. True prayer is not too much self-examination and striving for self-improvement, for then we are more concerned with evil or what we feel is "not good" than with God. Prayer is not working out our troubles but it is returning to God.

Our prayers have been too long, too wordy, with too much concern for their form. Prayer should never include thoughts and feelings against yourself. Never enter prayer with unforgiveness, hate, hurt, judgment, or revenge in your heart. Such thoughts and feelings hamper your ability to release your own God-power.

Prayer is not *many words*, and then complete unbelief. If the answer to prayer does not come at once, continue in your praise and thanksgiving, and whatsoever you have need of will manifest itself in its fullness. Prayer is not from the head alone but from the heart.

Prayer is not a *last-resort* idea. Every failure is a new opportunity for prayer. Prayer is too mighty and too wonderful to be used as a last resort. Prayers are not answered because you are good but because you merge into the consciousness of God's Presence.

YOU ARE IMPORTANT TO GOD

You who read this page, what are you? Why were *you* given the power to pray? You are the image and likeness of God. God is not a long way off; God is that which you call "I" and "me." Do you know this? You are so much more than you dare believe and yet, at this moment, something deep within you tells you how truly wonderful you are. Does it not? Even when you doubt yourself and are most fearful and ashamed, is there not something deep within you that defends you for *you know you are important to God?*

Is this dangerous teaching? To tell you who you really are? To tell you that you have power and authority? *Man's not knowing is his sin.* Man's not knowing has kept him in bondage, fear, and emptiness. Man has *not* been fired with an inner fire that would set free the great Spirit within him. In man's mind the door has been closed between himself and his indwelling Spirit. Man has been deadened by an opiate of "not knowing" that has reacted like a sleeping sickness, that has caused him to be unaware of his true self, of this captive Spirit that is within him.

You have only one goal in life: through your conscious awareness of God-in-you and your complete cooperation, to bring forth or fulfill what you already are!

God-in-you is your natural talent, your dearest desire, your fondest hope, your greatest plan, your most constant prayer. God-in-you is *what you want to be,* what you are striving to bring forth.

Right now God is your healing, your freedom, your right place, your abundance, your family's good. Whatever is uppermost in your heart and mind this moment is God pushing through you to fulfill your every desire.

Prayer is the recognition of your own true and wonderful self. Yes, this human outer self is the expression of God. The word "prayer" is a derivative of an ancient Sanskrit word *pal-al* which means "judging oneself as wondrously made." Prayer, then, is a constant song of praise of the wonder of God-in-you, his nearness, his power, his beauty, his wholeness.

PRAYER LETS YOU KNOW

Prayer does not change you; it only changes your mind from what you have thought you are to what you really are and have always been—a son of God.

Whoever you are, wherever you are today, the truth about you is that, *at this moment,* you are an expression of God at the very point at which you find yourself. This is your true expression. This is true of every soul and of every lesser creation. You cannot, by action, by thinking, or believing, change that which is true, *God in you.* But you can "not know" and by not knowing continue in unhappy, fearful conditions.

By the action of prayer *you can know.* You can know that this place where you find yourself is good—if *you,* with your lips and your heart, will acknowledge it and claim it with your words to be so. God is with you because He is unfolding in you your greatest good. Lift your voice in prayer, and accept *good only.*

To whom do you pray? "To God," you say. But *do* you?

We think we are praying to God, but sometimes we are expecting the answer to come through the doctor, the banker, a relative, or some outer power, or in a change of condition or environment. We sometimes hope that by some great stroke of luck we will receive what is needful. Often we wonder why our prayers are not answered.

They are not answered because this is not prayer. Prayer is always directed to God. God is the invisible Presence that created you and that lives in you this moment. Prayer is the action of your personal mind coupled with the God-mind, which moves through you and is the power that takes care of all things needful to your body and life. This God-power within you is greater than anything in the "outer." This is the Almighty God, the Good! It is through this invisible Substance, Energy, Power that all things are possible. Pray to God who creates, and is now creating, every living thing and who lives in that creation. Do not pray to any lesser power than the Almighty One.

WHY DO YOU PRAY?

Nothing is brought forth except by law. The law of growth, unfoldment, and fulfillment depends upon the law of the seed and upon you complying with this law. Prayer is the *seed* of *man*. Without seed there is nothing.

You pray to bring forth everything that you were created to bring forth.

You pray to know your self, your wonderful, glorious God-self, which is deep within you.

You pray to release the great substance of God that lies captive within you. This God-substance if *not* released cankers and spoils within you, affecting your health and life;

but if it is released, you will become radiant, strong, wise, and free.

Unused good becomes stagnant within you; many more people are suffering from unused good than from the need of good.

You pray to have the things that are needful. The thing you need is what the good God is trying to give to you. Prayer is power that brings everything forth. Prayer is establishing a pattern of mind so that we may see its fulfillment in our outer life. Prayer as praise and thanksgiving sets up the consciousness that opens the door for the outrush of man's good.

You pray for others in order to set your mind free from the thoughts you have about them. You pray for others that you may know the God-self of every man, that you may lift every man in your mind to his perfect being.

Why can you pray for and expect bodily healing? The healing law in man is as natural as his breathing, as natural as sleep. The Law of God as the Law of Life is constantly renewing itself, re-creating, rebuilding, at work at all times in all creation. Healing is natural and normal, for it is the principle of life. The restoring power in the body is *life* in its eternal action. We can let the healing life principle flow through us or we can interfere with it; which, depends on our thinking and established consciousness.

Sickness is not God's will for us, nor is it God punishing us. It is the result that comes because we have failed to accept in our mind the realization of this great Power that works easily and naturally through us, healing a cut finger or an incurable condition with equal ease. The moment we recognize and accept the law of healing within us, it is set free in our body to accomplish its perfect law.

Fear, worry, hate, unhappiness, criticism, all interfere with the perfect function of the law of healing. Prayer is the action by which man restores his conscious mind to its rightful relationship with the law of wholeness that is innate and natural to man.

Healing is simply *knowing* the truth of God's Presence as the life in our body and the power of our mind, and resting in the knowledge of this Presence. The normal, natural action of knowing that God's good is in us will heal every cell, organ, and function.

WHAT DOES PRAYER BECOME?

Prayer is progressive. Prayer becomes a way of life—wordless, living, true, and perfect. Ceaseless prayer becomes a pattern of consciousness expressed in everyday living.

Prayer becomes a conscious and constant relationship with the Creator of your being—a completion of the outer part of you and the true inner part of you that makes you a complete being. For this purpose you were created.

Prayer causes us to accept the responsibility of living—by letting our true identity come forth. To pray without ceasing is to have come to a moment-by-moment realization of God's presence at all times, in all places, with every experience and condition, and with all people.

Prayer brings about a knowing that needs no questioning, no directing—a fullness that fills the soul.

Prayer is not just association with God at a prayer time, but a constant at-one-ment, making every word a prayer, between prayers. What do you say between prayers? Do you nullify prayer with idle, negative, sick, unhappy talk? Watch the words of your everyday life.

NOW IS THE TIME TO PRAY

When do you pray? Pray while you read, walk, listen to music, while falling asleep or awakening. Pray in the bath. Pray while dressing or undressing. Pray in the elevator, in your car, in the bus, in the plane. Pray between interviews or sales. Pray with pencil and paper. Pray endlessly. Praise God from whom all blessings flow. Pray to know that prayer is always answered. Pray as though your prayer could change the world. Pray before you start, while you are in the midst, and after it has passed.

Do you want a better life? Do you want to have your soul fulfilled? Do you want to have a sense of well-being, a good feeling? Do you want to be well, happy, free, alive? Do you really? How much do you want these things? Enough to make an effort? Let me tell you a secret. You will never have them unless *you* want them enough to do something about them.

All receiving is *present tense*. There is no postponement. *Now is your time; you can do it*, whoever you are, wherever you are, regardless of your condition, situation, past, or present. Your good is at hand, but *you* must do something to achieve it, to bring it into visibility.

Prayer is the answer to man's every need. If you want all good, then pray.

If you do not know how to pray, learn to pray by praising and by giving thanks that you are always "kept" by your Creator.

If you know how to pray, may we inspire you to *join all mankind*? We want your prayer power with us for yourself and for the world. Prayer is something that every living soul should contribute to mankind. It is the greatest gift man can give.

We cannot say there is no time for prayer, no matter how busy our life may be. If we say this, we are saying, No time for God. We shut the door on health, happiness, joy, and fulfillment.

We do not need to be educated or trained for prayer.

Prayer is as simple as sowing seed; as natural as breathing; as easy as sleeping.

Do not pray in awe or superstition, but as easily as you would talk to a good friend or loved one.

Prayer is *for you*, not to change God or make God do something for you. Prayer is accepting the responsibility of living, realizing your true identity.

Let us pray to bring God's good world into view. Let us join the legions who are praying today, that the prayer power may swell and fill the earth.

Remember, it is never too late to pray. With God all things are possible. With the Almighty there is no incurable, impossible situation or condition, but you must lift yourself through prayer to the God-mind.

Why should every living soul pray?

It is imperative for every living soul to pray because we are all God-in-expression; we must *press* Him forth through us. Man has brought forth his present world of sickness, lack, hate, war, and confusion because there was something he did not know. Man has not kept his awareness of God because he has not known God lives, moves, and has His being in him and in all. In this knowledge lies all freedom.

We have believed there is a Supreme Presence somewhere, but we have not believed ourselves worthy to house this Presence; much less have we *known that we are this Presence*.

The same Power is in us all. Can you pray for every other human being because you know there was only *one man* created and that *man* is in us all? Can you pray for your enemies and those that spitefully use you? Can you pray for every stranger, near and far? If you *can* and *will*, you will be blessed.

HOW TO PRAY

Close your eyes. How can you contact that which is in you unless you close your eyes? Now, think of the situation or condition that is untenable for you—the thing that you cannot live with for another moment. You don't want to be sick. You don't want to fail. In your mind think of whatever it is—walk right up to it. This is the lion that you meet on your path. Walk right up to it and face it.

Within your heart you have said, "O God, can't you release me from this? Can't you take this cup from my lips?" If you have any situation, of any kind, at any level, wherein you feel you can't go forward another day, think about the situation for just one moment. (You are thinking about it all the time anyway, so it won't be very hard to think about it again, right now.)

I want you to *let go of it now*. Just lay it aside for one moment—this moment—and think about God, the joy of fulfillment, well-being, good feeling, your right place; your mind eased, the release. Get the warm feeling of anticipation: "I have the letter." "I have the position." "I have the healing." The minute you start thinking about these things, your body vibrates with them. Now, I know your old fears are not going to let you have that good feeling very long. They will be right back, saying, "But you know you are too old. You know you can't. . . ."

Do it again if these things come back and try to crowd in on you. Just for one moment, again put them aside and get this warm feeling, this anticipation of your good. It will desert you again and again and again. Never mind; lay it aside—that which would rob you—again and again and again. For if you have been able for one second to let go of that which worries you, it is absolute *proof* that you can let go of it altogether and move forward to your highest good.

Praise and give thanks that God is fulfilling your greatest need—now *say* it, *say* it, *say* it, and you will see it come forth in all its glory.

Remember, God cannot do anything for you or through you *without* you. *You must give your mind—it is up to you.* If you do not have your good it will be because you did not want it enough to pray. But you do want your good, don't you?

"Men ought always to pray, and not to faint" (Luke 18:1) . . . for I know *that, even now,* whatsoever you will ask of God, God will give it thee (John 11:22).

WHY SAY "AMEN"?

We say "Amen." Amen means certainly, true, so be it, verily, I approve, I accept, I am faithful and it will be certain.

The whole meaning and power of prayer depends on your acceptance or "signature." It is your signature that makes it authentic. Your signature on a paper in the outer world signifies your intention, your acceptance. It is a sign from you. It is your wish and command made known.

"Amen" is the sign that you are now ready to accept your good. You have assigned or conveyed the authority to God.

"Amen" is a sign that incites action. It is the acceptance in your heart and mind of something eminent, memorable, and extraordinary.

When you say "Amen," do you know that you are filing notice of intent, you are making your signature, and that until you do this God has no power to make you accept the good that you were created to express.

"Amen" means you have accepted God's promise—the

promise of *good* with you always—in spite of everything, in view of every indication to the contrary.

Our good is certain but *our acceptance* is the doubtful part.

We say "Amen" without any idea that it is a thousand times more powerful and binding than our name on a note at the bank. It is a magic word and the power of the true "Amen" will be a power when all banks are closed and man's economic system has fallen into nothingness.

Above all, this is the Law of Life. Man must accept the good of God. When we accept the good and needful things of God in our heart and mind, we are believing, and the promise is "All things are possible to him that believeth" (Mark 9:23).

9. Meet Yourself

In the experiences of life, we feel so alone. Perhaps an inner loneliness is the most prevalent condition in men and women. This does not mean that we are alone in the outer world; we may be in the midst of a crowd and be receiving much attention, yet feel alone in the innermost part of us. This loneliness is much deeper than surface conditions and appearances; it is an inner emptiness, an inner hunger that must be filled.

We are all compulsory witnesses to life. We are here, and one of the deepest lessons the human soul can learn is that we must keep on living; we must go on. Experience is the pattern of life and every occurrence is the unfoldment of a higher state of knowing and believing. We must know that every happening of life is part of our development and growth, that it is not failure or God punishing us.

If we feel alone, it is because we have not reconciled our outer self with life and its pattern unfolding through us. We should get "something" from every experience, whether it appears to be good, bad, or indifferent. This is referred to in Scripture: "I will not let you go, except thou bless me" (Gen. 32:26). All roads lead to our highest good and all assignments in life are for our richest unfoldment, regardless of appearances or our human judgment about them.

LIFE IS TO BE MET

Most of us are searching for God here, there, and everywhere—in books, in organizations, in other people. We are trying to make ourselves over when in truth there is nothing to change, only something to know. All change is really further unfoldment of that which already is. We are not told that we must change the world and then we shall be free; we are told that we shall know the truth and we shall be free. We must know who and what we are; we must understand that the pattern of life is made up of many changing events. The Power within us will not let us rest until we accomplish our goal, so we cannot fail; but we can be unaware of what is happening to us and so miss the joy of the experience.

We are compelled to take each moment of life as it comes. We try to keep from having difficulties, challenges, troubles. We think we have failed if these come to us, but the truth is that we fail when we do not *move forward* to meet the events as they appear. We usually work against ourselves because we do not give ourselves to the happenings of life. That we do not move with life is our greatest failure and it causes the most unhappiness. We are fearful to step out of the little personal pattern of life that we have built, like a child builds a house of blocks. Our small expression of limitless life, however great it may appear to us, no more resembles our destiny than night resembles day. "It is the Father's good pleasure to give you the Kingdom" (Luke 12:32). God is forever directing us to our highest expression, even when we think we are directing ourselves. The great Power within pushes through us as desire and need.

By devious paths the indwelling Power leads us; through other people it beckons us; by the longing of our heart it draws us. All of us, however small our field of activity, must have individual supremacy in our own soul and dynamic evidence or proof positive to ourselves that we are worth while, that we have something special to contribute to the world. Life then becomes the way by which we make this contribution.

All experiences are opportunities to prove ourselves. Search every place, every face, every happening, for good. Establish in yourself a core of faithfulness so that whatever happens you are carried through by your own conscious knowing. Every experience has its overshadowing good. We are to prove this good. "Prove me now" is the command; as a singer must sing, a scientist explore, so must we find good in the mysterious ways of life. The inner Power always appears in times of great stress. It is a terrible thing to be caught in growth and not to grow, for growth is our destiny.

Martin Luther said, "God is a blank sheet upon which nothing is found but what you yourself have written." As human beings, we have not the words to frame our loftiest dreams, but we have feelings that swell within us to bring them forth. We say we do not know what we should do but the truth is, we do not listen to our hearts and we do not know ourselves. As God-beings walking an earthly path, we are a great contradiction.

THE GREAT CONTRADICTION

We talk about the hopelessness of life, and in almost the same breath declare the things we hope to accomplish. We talk about God as All-Power, and then talk freely of things we refer to as "incurable" and "impossible." Scripture tells us that God is all and God is good, but we talk about the evil that abounds everywhere. We forget that evil is simply not knowing the law and principle of life, and that good is the result of knowing and abiding in truth, either in awareness or unawareness. We talk about peace and love, then listen attentively to reports on war and hate until our minds are saturated with them. We talk about how much we love, honor, and respect others, and then talk about the many things they are doing that are not to our liking. We talk about high prices, taxes, and what we can't afford, and then wonder why things are the way they are with us. We are well-read, well-educated, with much experience, but we do not understand the power of our own minds. We do not know that all things in the world are brought about through the action of mind. We are not always aware while we are talking that we are making our world and the very situations in which we ourselves must live.

States of consciousness are built by words—words that are read, spoken, and heard, and our lives are built by consciousness. If we would change results in our lives, we must look to ourselves. The physical body responds to words; blood rushes to our head when we are embarrassed. Cold perspiration breaks out and our legs become like jelly at even the calling of our name under certain circumstances. Isaiah tells us, "My word . . . shall not return unto me void, but it shall accomplish that which I please, and it shall prosper in the thing whereto I sent it" (55:11). Therefore, if we are to know ourselves, we must be conscious of our word.

We must know how important we are to ourselves and to all mankind. We must know that to be human is a grand and wonderful achievement, and that to be a real human being is to be God-in-expression. We have an inner self to honor and an inner freedom, but we are not always balanced in the circumstances that are happening around us. We must keep in balance between our outer self and our inner being, not be torn between them. We must believe in the presence of God in the midst of our humanity.

The difficulty with the human mind is that it wants to know how, when, and where. These are the eternal questions in man's mind. All life is a movement forward and upward whether we recognize it or not. We cannot even tarry very long, for life demands this traveling. To be delayed constantly by trying to know everything with exactness is a hindrance to our growth and maturity. Man's desire to know every step ahead is an obstruction and an interruption, and it causes many delays and much self-imposed suffering. There is an old saying, "When you cannot trace, trust." Scripture tells us, "Faith is the *substance of things hoped for*, the evidence of *things not seen*" (Heb. 11:1). Every human being must walk by faith for there is no other way. Nothing is guaranteed in life except the vision that comes as the beginning and the promise that we will be sustained and arrive at our destination. Moment-by-moment living is man's project and the outer pattern of his life.

God takes care of each one of us on this seemingly perilous journey of life. To believe this and to trust it is "the truth that sets us free."

DO NOT INTERFERE WITH YOUR OWN GOOD

Let us accept this gracious gift, the truth of our safety in God, and be free forever from haunting fear, loneliness, and indecision. God takes care of us and all people in every walk of life without question or discrimination. We are only required to *know* it. You must accept this without understanding just *how* God will do it; since you cannot perceive directly, you must know that this Power in you can and will.

Strange as it may seem, the moment you begin to try to know how the law of good is going to work, your human mind shuts off the free flow of good. The important thing is to go about doing whatever lies at hand, trusting that this good will come forth for you, and your believing will make it so.

It is given to you to stand at the beginning and know the end, but *how* life is going to carry you through each day and just what experiences you must meet is *not* revealed to you. You are directed from within and you must know the promise is made to whosoever "shall not doubt in his heart he shall have whatsoever he saith" (Mark 11:23). Know that you are being directed to your highest good and it shall be completed.

The detailed thinking of the mind is reserved for bringing forth the outer material things of our world. The invisible expression of life—our inner relationship with ourselves and others, our loves, our hopes, our reactions and feelings—must be directed from an inner guidance, not from outer thinking.

We live and express ourselves in this world with many distractions, pulls, hates, and misunderstandings brought about by ignorance. We know there is warmth, love, and goodness in this world that radiates out of the hearts of men and women and re-echoes in our own. There is joy and happiness and many wonderful things but much of the time these wonderful things are overshadowed by our doubts and fears. We are afraid, somehow, that our good can be lost or that something we love can be destroyed.

Let us go back to the Truth, that we must know just as we are that we are held securely by the law and principle of life, but we must use this principle. When you look at the outer world, you see all its human problems, the unspeakable things that are happening, the mental and physical sickness that abounds, the poverty and lack that makes beggars of us all, and the state of affairs that appears on the screen of life.

There is a greater truth than all of these. Jesus said, "Judge not according to the appearance, but judge righteous judgment" (John 7:24). There is in the mind and heart of man a power that is greater than "he that is in the world" (John 4:4). With his mind and in ignorance of the Law, man has built a fantastic outer world; with this same mind and with knowledge of the Law, he can build a new world. "A new heaven and a new earth" (Rev. 21:1) is the prophecy. This power is set in motion by the power of believing and knowing. Scripture says, "Shall not doubt in his heart but shall believe" (Mark 11:23). To fulfill and sustain us is God's business; believing and knowing is our business.

Whatever you fear, you are greater than your adversary. Whatever it is that is trying to take command of you, *you have command over it*, at all times, "if you can believe" (Mark 9:23). To paraphrase Matthew (8:9), you have the power to say, "Go, and it goeth; come, and it cometh." Your believing sustains everything that is in your life. No condition or situation can stand for you without the invisible support of your mind.

We are often so overcome by our problems and situations that we are numb with fear. These things in life are so real, and to be free of them so seemingly impossible, that we do not even lift our hand or our mind against them. We just submit to them. Sin is separation; it comes from an old word that means missing the mark. Our sin is one of omission; we do not keep our oneness with good uppermost in mind and we submit to and accept as inevitable conditions and situations.

If, without questioning *how*, you can *know* that this Power within can do all things, all power is yours. But if your little mind wants to know how a healing can be accomplished when the wisdom of man has said it is incurable, if it must know *how* God can set us free from bondage, if your mind must work out reasons for everything, then the Power does not work for you.

Do you belittle yourself or allow anyone else to belittle you? This is to trespass on God. Do not be awed by the things of the "outer." The wise man is awed by the invisible, by the things he cannot understand. This invisible Power within him is like radium, for it gives off an eternal and deathless energy, never changes, and can do all things.

We have drawn from others in the past, but the time is at hand when no man will be satisfied until *he feels this great Power within himself and rests in it* and lets it work through him.

While we do not *know how* this tremendous Power of God can heal broken bodies, broken hearts, broken lives, and broken dreams, we must know that God is unfolding in all, and to know this is enough. This is all we need to know.

Right now you may need to be healed, yet you cannot understand, and the wisest man does not understand, how organs and cells are renewed and re-created. But *you must know that they are.*

If you can *know* without inquiring *how* with your little mind, *you have stepped into the Kingdom of Heaven* and "all . . . things shall be added unto you" (Luke 12:31; Matt. 6:33). Everything in the universe is order and precision. The turning of the earth, the ebb and flow of the tides, the stars in the sky, and the seasons are definite and true. Only we defy the divine order, simply because we do not know. We must know that this same Power is the Law of Life and of our being and that we can trust it. "With God all things are possible" (Matt. 19:26; Mark 10:27).

10. The Death of Death

Holy days are holidays—days of exemption from the cares of life, release from labor and work. We keep these holy days with undeviating regularity, for deep within us they have some great cosmic meaning, something that does not yet touch the surface of our outer mind and everyday life.

To millions of people, Easter is a holiday. To many it is also a holy day. Why do we remember this day?

At every Eastertime, down through the centuries, the joyful cry has been heard, "He is risen! He is risen!"

Jesus came that man might have life and, according to events, raised Lazarus from the dead just a week before he met his own fulfillment when he triumphed over those who killed him. Now, three days later, the tomb was empty!

What makes this story so important? What makes this day so different? Why, almost two thousand years later, do people gather on Easter in commemoration of this man and what He accomplished?

What was His message and why is it so important to every

man? His message is *about* every man. It carries the truth of man's own being. In it, Jesus reveals to every man, man's own divinity and reminds man that there is in every human form, a Power and a Presence that directs and sustains that living soul always.

He tells every man that all things are possible to man in heaven and on earth, if he will recognize and call forth this indwelling Power. This was His message then, and this is His message now—"the same yesterday, today, and forever."

What are they celebrating on Easter? Why are they rejoicing? They are celebrating Jesus' triumph—the death of death. Yes, *the death of death*.

Death has always been man's arch enemy, the grim reaper of life, the thief of babe, of child, of those in the fullness of life as well as those who have lived long. It is the enemy of enemies and, our Scripture tells us, "the last enemy that shall be destroyed" (I Cor. 15:26).

Death was destroyed by One who put all things under His dominion, and walked in peace and power because he recognized that God *is All in all*.

Death is dead! It is the reassurance of eternal life on earth. Your reasoning mind says, "You must be joking. This isn't meant for *us*. It can't mean modern man. We understand life and death, and death is inevitable."

Easter is the name of the old Teutonic goddess of Spring. Easter and Spring come with the vernal equinox. Let us learn to listen and to be aware of this annual message of Spring. The fragrance of the flowers fills the air to remind us that God has again renewed his covenant with man. Every seed is stirring, every bud is swelling. Every bulb in the warm earth and every blade of grass answers the call. Every heart is quickened with new life.

It is the resurrection of the earth. It is the resurrection of all that is hidden in it and all that grows upon it. Let us the answer. The lifting of the body to a new vibration by a new approach to life is the hope of man.

Man knows, without a doubt in his mind, that death must come to him, and as he believes so shall it be with him. This is the power of man's mind. He has even decided that there must be great wars to thin out the great population explosion. He proclaims that death must live to give man his opportunity. His opportunity for what? To live? Or, an opportunity to die? Man carries on senseless chatter. "Who wants to live?" he asks. *You* want to live, man, *you do*, and you alone must find this answer in your hearts.

Deep down in our souls, we all want life. Every movement of our mind and soul is to ensure life. We may say, "I don't want to live on this earth, in this body with pain and discomfort, helpless and old," but we all want life some way, somehow. Of course we don't want an eternal nightmare; this is not *life*.

Man is still searching for the Fountain of Youth, some elixir of life, that he may be transfigured. Not just a shoddy idea of staying young but a fulfillment, a transformation, that is promised in hundreds of scriptures. That which we are to have is the fruits of righteousness. Righteousness is a right approach to life in our hearts and minds, a right relationship with one another and with ourselves. We are to love and to exercise a new attitude in life. "Let all bitterness and wrath, and anger, and clamor, and evil speaking be put away from you, with all malice" (Eph. 4:31).

The work that must be done is in our minds and in our attitude to life. We cannot hate and live.

The greatest promise of all is, "You shall know the truth, and the truth shall set you free" (John 8:32). "I will ransom them from the power of the grave; I will redeem them from death" (Hos. 13:14).

Let's not fool ourselves. We want to live but we want a

life that is transformed, a body that is illumined with power. We long for death because we believe that we are going to have new life.

But man's failure has been in believing that he can escape from life and not fulfill the Law of Life in his everyday world, here and now. The book of Law says, "I have set before you life and good, and death and evil; . . . therefore choose life that . . . you . . . may live" (Deut. 30:15, 19). We want to live in the fullness of life. This is our deepest desire. Let us hold fast to this desire, for it is from God.

We may be caught on the wheel of life and death; I may not overcome it, you may not overcome it, but we can start now to contribute to its overcoming in our power to believe and see the change in our individual lives.

All doctors, scientists, and those who do research are on this very path. Every new idea is a step on the way. Those who search *believe* in their hearts that the answer is there, because unsuspectingly they too believe in life eternal.

All mankind will find the secret of life again, because *one man found it*. When the secret of life is found, it will be because many believed.

Soundlessly the great Truth moves through the minds and hearts of men and women. Those who think and feel deeply know that death is not man's true destiny.

Although man tries to make peace with death, to resign himself to it, still he appeals to all the faith that he can muster, and he holds to the goodness of God and to his oneness with God. Man compromises with death, he concedes, but this concession is not final, nor has he accepted it in his heart and soul. Life continues to flow through him until he must accept it in its fullness here and now.

In man's reasoning about and trying to understand death, which in the end is not understandable, he has relegated this eternal life to some state that he will enter after death.

But the words of Jesus are clear and true, and it would be very difficult to twist them to mean something else: "If a man keep my saying, he shall never see death" (John 8:51).

But this is how man reasons: "How could man live on earth if there were no death?" The masses of people, the problem of food and fresh water, he argues and he reasons. "How could man live?" I do not know, but I do know that there is a Power, a great Intelligence that created this earth and man, and perhaps created death as an escape for man until he can come into his majority, his own true greatness. This Power is capable of bringing forth and maintaining life, for this is its whole purpose.

MAN MUST CHANGE

There is a Power that created this earth and filled it with glory and beauty and wonder. *It is man who must change.*

This world is a pinpoint in the universe, of which the immense galaxy in which our earth spins is only a tiny part. There are billions of spheres unknown and only faintly dreamed of by man. Man's mind and its limitations are not the outer limits of God's world or of the universe. Man is an infant, playing in his little mind with the reaches of infinity. He has no conception, not even a glimmer, of the vastness of this universe to which he as man belongs.

The death of death—how can it be? *It cannot be in the limitations of man's mind.*

But it is already, some way, somehow, beyond his present understanding; it is the true plan of every man. Already the mind of man yearns for and is even now building the way as he sends forth the first explorers into the realms of space.

It may be that the answer to the population explosion and the needs of man on earth will be found in the skies.

Surely we are on the verge of great and far-reaching revelations and accomplishments.

But one thing is certain: *Man must change.* He must be ready for the things that the Scriptures foretell—wonders of life and love. "Eye hath not seen, nor ear heard, neither have entered into the heart of man, the things which God hath prepared for them that love him" (I Cor. 2:9).

Perhaps someday we shall know what it means in Genesis where it says ". . . when men began to multiply on the face of the earth, . . . the sons of God saw the daughters of men that they were fair; and they took them wives of all which they chose. . . . There were giants in the earth in those days . . . when the sons of God came in unto the daughters of men, and they bare children to them, the same became mighty men which were of old, men of renown" (6:1, 2, 4).

It may be that the lifeblood of those of the earth must again be infused with that of the sons of God so that man may be renewed. We need giants on earth that can be "the mighty men of renown." The new life may come in a mysterious way so that the creation of God may be fair and beautiful again.

Perhaps you cannot dream my dream but you can dream your own dream. Dream you must, for "Where there is no vision, the people perish" (Prov. 29:18). There is no end to that which is eternal. God is limitless, omnipresent, omniscient, and omnipotent. There is no end to a God that fills the earth and the universe of universes. We are a part of all that is, of all that can ever be. We come "from afar: not in entire forgetfulness, and not in utter nakedness, but trailing clouds of glory do we come from God, who is our home" (Wordsworth).

We are only beginning to comprehend dimly the meaning of the priceless gift of life. Can we not trust an all-powerful God? Can we not trust a God that moves in the very being of every man with a movement that, at this time, man does not understand, or believe himself worthy of knowing or finding? The Power of all Powers dwells in man himself.

The secret is not given to the baby or to the small child, nor to the callous youth who moves through the cruelest aspect of life, having yet no refinement or feelings for others. It is not revealed to the man or woman whose mind and throat are filled with the dust of the earth, with fear and a need of the bread and butter of life, or caught in the quicksand of the activities of his neighbor and the evildoing of the world.

How can this man "whose breath is in his nostrils" (Isa. 2:22) know that which is knowable only to a man who knows his very breath *is God?* If man has no comprehension or awareness that a Power takes care of him in the least as well as the greatest moments of his life, then he has missed God.

We must know that when we are alone or when we are in a crowd, when we are beset on every side or when peace reigns within and penetrates and fills every cell of our bodies, always we are in the care and keeping of our Creator.

If we do not accept our Creator's care and protection in the everyday walks of life, in every moment of growth and unfoldment, in sickness, in health, in our eating, in clothing ourselves, in work and in play, how can we ever envision or accept the fact that God can take care of us in the farthest reaches of space?

That this Power is with us, has always been with us in the eons and eons of development through which we have come, is the Truth of God. All that still lies before us, beyond the limits of our earth and our misty conception of our heavens, is God-given.

A challenge comes to us in the words of the One who walked the way of death and of eternal life, spoken to all who will believe: "I say unto you, he that believeth on me, the works that I do shall he do also; and greater works than these shall he do" (John 14:12). We cannot understand this promise because we have not yet been able to heal the sick, raise the dead, feed five thousand, or still the storm in the hearts of men and establish peace on earth. What could Jesus have meant? What greater works than these could we do?

Jesus healed the people of the conditions resulting from their unknowing. Our greater work could be to root out and eliminate the *cause* of hunger, turmoil, sickness, and death, so there would be nothing to heal. We have been lost in what Jesus did instead of doing the greater things that he declared we might do. "Ye shall know the truth and the truth shall set you free" (John 8:32). This is our destiny.

Are we to fulfill our destiny or are we to return to the dust? Do we dream up these dreams alone, or through them are we touched and inspired by some power on high? Or is it the Power moving in our minds and hearts that urges us on and on?

When Easter morning comes and goes do we sink back in the lethargy of the ages? Will you slumber with your fathers or will you answer the call? "Because I live, you shall live also." . . . "I am come that they might have life, and that they might have it more abundantly"—that you may come up out of death. "Destroy this temple, and in three days I will raise it up" (John 14:19; 10:10; 2:19).

Will you answer the call? He is saying: "I have left you an empty tomb. Why do you go on filling tombs? I brought the great gift of life for all who follow me, for all who live after me!"

Does your human mind answer, "Not me, not me. This is too great for me. I am only flesh and blood, a human being full of sin and corruption. I know that I am nothing because I tell myself every day of my nothingness." No matter what my soul says or how my heart cries out, I cannot accept what I cannot understand. I'm too smart for that. I know too much. A power that takes care of me? I take care of myself. I know that sickness, death, and lack of every kind are real. Maybe you think death is dead, but not for me."

Does your human mind continue, "Death may be the *last* enemy overcome, but I'm not willing to let go of this hate, this resentment, this hurt feeling, this hurt pride, this unkind deed. Hunger and poverty stalk my path but I will not accept the 'bread of heaven' or 'the living waters.' I know what bread costs, and even a drink of water is not free any more. What kind of fool do you take me for? Eternal life, peace, plenty—in this world, on this earth, at this time? No, 'I do not believe.' "

BELIEVING IS THE SECRET

The answer is, we do not believe. Why are things the way they are with man? Man does not believe in the goodness of God, much less in any goodness in man. Man just doesn't believe—and *we are that man.* We will only accept what we can believe or accept as probable with our human minds. *We do not live because we do not believe.* We will not see beyond what we can see or feel, beyond what we feel should be felt. If we will not see or think or believe beyond what passes before the eye, we "shall surely die."

God is in this world and moving in the hearts and minds of men and women. Those who feel his movement are going forward into the unknown. These are the "remnant," the "elect," the Scriptures speak of. Because of these, some shall enjoy the wealth of the Kingdom. Others shall sit outside and deny that there is such a place, for they will not go in and see for themselves.

There is a heaven on earth, but no one can enjoy it who

does not find it and go in. The passport is faith believing. Are you a part of the new world, the new heaven, and the new earth? Or *is the good of God too good for you?*

Are you too wise to fall into the trap of believing in God? Scripture tells us, "It is a fearful thing to fall into the hands of the living God" (Heb. 10:31), for you will have to sacrifice all your old beliefs, your fears, your cocksure opinions, or any state of mind that separates you from your Creator.

This message of life was not just for Christians, for there were no so-called Christians in that day. It was for Jew and Gentile alike, and for Roman and Greek. At the birth of Jesus, the angels told the shepherds that the glad tidings of life were *for all men always.* The whole world needs the message of life, for there are, and always have been, Jewish boys, Christian boys, Buddhist boys dying side by side. This is not a heritage for any one segment of mankind. This is the gift of God to every man.

The death of death! The human mind reasons on: "What about medicine and all the modern doctors and their wonders?" These too are a part of the way. This is the search man's mind is making because he knows there must be a way.

Every path leads to God; every step is a step on the way. It is an uphill fight, for all that doctors and science can do, man with his fear, hate, unhappiness, loneliness, and injustice can undo. Man is thwarted by himself.

The path of life is a path of peace in the heart and mind of every man. Eternal life is the good of man. "It can never be," the unbeliever cries. "There would not be enough food. The earth and all that is upon it would perish." No, the earth is but a speck in the universe. There is much room and man will always find a way. He is even now pondering it and he will find it.

The way is here already. Only man is not ready for the way.

The further secrets of life will not be revealed until man comprehends the gift of life and peace that was given to him in the cool of the morning of that first Easter. It was given us by that One who found the way and followed it, and who said, "Follow me." Let us know that "me" is within each of us.

Where is the way? We must go within, for it is an inner path found only in the mind and heart of man. The inner way is the only way that leads to power. This path within leads to new life and reveals the ideas that lead to freedom.

The revelation of the wisdom of the ages and the breakthrough of modern man on all frontiers signal the awakening of all mankind. Man is being set free from the wheel of pain and suffering on which he has turned for so long. Man was bound to the wheel because he insisted that the way he had to walk was the way of the world outside himself.

Through ideas comes all that sustains man, and man has a hidden wealth in this storehouse of power within. These ideas will come forth to fit any emergency and to fill any need. Man will have ideas that will carry him every step of the unknown way. Ideas will come that stem from an inner knowing. This path is for every man on the face of the earth.

When man is willing to share his "path of progress" with every living soul, regardless of race, color, creed, education, station in life, differences or likenesses, he will find all power. Until we know that we cannot go into true life and freedom alone, but must carry all of humanity in our hearts and minds—until we know this, we will remain apart.

When we are ready in our hearts, then shall the way open up before us. Every step will be an adventure if we are willing to follow the path *all the way*. To be ready means individual preparation, for the only door that opens onto the way is a hidden door in the heart and mind of each man. But the promise is that "you shall seek me, and find me, when you shall search for me with all your heart" (Jer. 29:13). This comes when you are willing.

"Why seek ye the living among the dead?" The old world, the old way, of war, greed, and hate is dead. Even the old world of the goodness of God that has always moved in the hearts and minds of all men in the restricted area of "me and mine" is dead.

We must include our fellow men. "And I saw a new heaven and a new earth: for the first heaven and the first earth were passed away; . . . and there shall be no more death" neither sorrow, nor crying, neither shall there be any more pain, for the former things have passed away (Rev. 21:1, 4). This means here and now for you and your fellow man. The catch is, "Do ye now believe?" (John 16:31).

Yes, death is dead but man hasn't found it out yet. The first Easter was the death of death for all mankind. Scripture tells us that "some doubted" (Matt. 28:17). Perhaps men of this age cannot, at this point, accept eternal life, but deep in their hearts beyond the doubt they are beginning to know that more is possible than they have ever dreamed.

After Jesus had witnessed the death of death for himself, He said to the doubters: "Peace be unto you. . . . Why are you troubled? and why do thoughts rise in your hearts? . . . Blessed are they that have not seen, and yet have believed" (Luke 24:36, 38; John 20:29).

Death is dead. *Can you believe?*

11. Life Is the Activity of God

We have entered into the physical being for a very special purpose—to "bear witness to the truth" (John 18:37). The urge in man to complete his soul is the greatest drive on earth, and by this impelling force all things are carried forward. No human being can fail to make this completion, regardless of his human measure of failure or success, for it is an inner achievement and cannot be judged by appearances. "There is no power but of God." "With God all things are possible" (Rom. 13:1; Matt. 19:26).

All advancement is made by man as he continues on this quest. The advancement is incidental; the search is the thing. The millions of material things that fill our world are the by-products of this seeking; the seeking goes on and on. No generation can convince another that the search is over. No individual, by his experience and knowledge, can persuade or stay another from the need to move on. No one, with his own unbelief or dispairing tale of failure and frustration, can deter another. The poet tells us that that which we seek is within us, "closer than our breath." Why, then, do we seek?

We seek because we have not yet *experienced* it. The Spirit of God has not taken us over. We are talking about this indwelling power, locating it, reminding ourselves of its great power and ability, its wonder, its peace, but *we have not given it freedom* to guide our mind and life.

We must experience the meaning of the words of Jesus when He said, "I can of mine own self do nothing" (John 5:30). We must come to a place where, finally, we are able to let the innermost part of our heart and mind dictate the policies of life, not the reasoning, probing mind of worldly loss and gain. Then, and then only, will we be set free from worry, fear, and anxiety about ourselves, our life, and others. We will then have *time to live* as God created us to live, with *power and authority*. We shall have life "more abundantly."

Many have ceased searching and are despondent. They have stopped short of their *goal. They have stopped short of God.*

Freedom is the divine right of every living soul. If we do not have it, it is our own fault. Freedom is release from anything that hampers and keeps us from our good. True freedom is to fulfill our destiny.

What would you give to be free from some condition or situation that seems unbearable or untenable? Are you willing to give up fear-thoughts and to reverse your negative opinions? To move on?

We want our good to happen to us. We want to be completely aware and conscious of *our own indwelling God.* This is our divine right. We want *our* good life, *our* success, *our* well-being. We don't want to enjoy our good vicariously. We are tired of *hearing about* happiness, joy, success, freedom, and health. We *want* them.

We are weary of being onlookers, of watching things taking place in other people's lives and in the movies. We want things to happen to *us* and we have a right to expect them. We are not meant to participate in other people's happiness, peace, and power to the exclusion of our own.

We have been told that unless we become "as a little child," we shall not enter the Kingdom of God which is the kingdom of good. When we think of great people, we think of those with great learning, prestige, material success, fame, fortune. We look to these things instead of to that which makes for true greatness—childlikeness. We have lost the sense of the wonder of things; as adults, we try to reduce all the beautiful and the wonderful to mediocrity. We want all things to be ordinary and explainable to human consciousness. Only the child believes in fairies, elves, trolls, and that all things can happen; grown-ups know better because they have adulterated their minds in the school of appearances. As a child, I believed in a guardian angel because over my bed there hung a picture of one watching over a little child gathering a flower on a precipice. Then I forgot, until I came back into an awareness that the guardian angel is the mysterious Presence that is with us always. Albert Einstein said, "The most beautiful thing we can experience is the mysterious, to know what is impenetrable really exists, manifesting itself as the highest wisdom and the most radiant beauty. This knowledge, this feeling, is the center of true religiousness."

We must believe in what our heart expects though it is yet hidden, believe in the real, the mystical, the fantastic turn of life that so often lies just beyond our faith.

The faith that the Scriptures honor is the natural instinct of a child, which is in perfect balance between two worlds. This kind of faith was the Hebrew heritage of men like Moses and Jesus, a living, vibrant faith that could carry them through impossible situations unscathed. Let us try to recapture our childlike faith.

A child is dependent and trusting until adult unworthiness breaks the trust. A child is friendly and unconscious of rank, color, or race. A king's child could play happily with a ragamuffin until the prejudice of the adult entered in. A child lives in constant wonder, imagines, and improvises; makes toys out of bits of glass and trash; and finds life a high romance. A child is candid and honest; go to a child if you want the truth. It is almost impossible to get the truth from an adult who must always fulfill the conventions and who seeks subterfuge in words.

A child expects great things in this world and is always filled with wonder. He is receptive to the joy of life. Childlikeness is the luster of the pearl of great price.

We have insulted the Creator of the universe with our petty theories and pompous opinions. We have drawn all our conclusions from the world outside us, from what appears to be.

Emerson said, in his "Essay on Compensation," "Things refuse to be mismanaged long." The time has come to accept "a more excellent way" (I Cor. 12:31) which is the new and living way. We sometimes think that we run a little world of our own, but it is in vain that we try to work against the law of God. The great directing Power is in us, so let us find the new way.

As striving human beings, we have tried every path. We have believed that the "touch of gold" would make us free, but with cold material good there is no freedom. We have tried the "touch of drugs," only to find ourselves caught in a mental and physical morass which becomes a living hell. We have tried the "touch of work," and worn out our bodies to no avail. We have tried to "do good," only to end frustrated and sometimes hated because of our endeavors. Finally, but with sure conviction, we are finding that the "touch of God" is the only answer, one that lies within the mind and heart of man. The "touch of God" is so simple. It comes about when we acknowledge our oneness with God, and know that we are worthy to accept our good. When we acknowledge our oneness with God, let us hold fast until this awareness becomes alive in us.

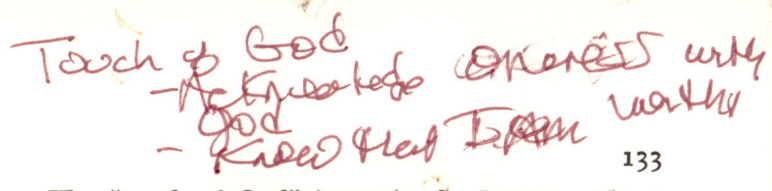

HOW DO WE DO IT?

Our goal is God. Our individual goal is to find within our own soul our own true self. Let us release all preconceived ideas about ourselves. Let go of the mistakes of the past and all those who have gone before us, and know that it is our stand, here and now, our consciousness and awareness, that the world needs. We must be ready and willing to step forth into this great drama of life and take every step that lies before us.

Let us accept ourselves. Accept this self that God has given you of Himself. Accept your background, race, color, parents; accept your heritage in life. Be proud of the path that you have traveled to come to this, the present day.

Do not say, "I am not good enough, I have made mistakes." How can you accept the great unfolding, unknown God if you can't accept yourself? Accept, and know you are not the same person you were yesterday and that you will not be the same tomorrow or the day after. Self-acceptance is the gateway to freedom and power.

Accept yourself without criticism, for we have all come by devious paths to this point in life. Do not look to the way you have come, which is behind you; that you are here is the only thing of importance. Do not accept the testimony of your conscious mind. It has been called "the great adversary, the devil, a liar and the Father of liars." Understand, you cannot accept the evidence of the outer world and its ever-changing mirage, for it is illusory and deceiving. Say to your human mind the words of the Psalmist, "Be still, and know that I am God" (Psalm 46:10).

Don't apologize for yourself, for unless you accept yourself you postpone your good. Don't say, "I could be better." Just say, "Here I am." Watch your human mind, for it will always make a plea for you—an alibi. You don't need this. You already are, and have always been, and there is "nothing good or bad but thinking makes it so." There are many things about life that you cannot explain or understand. Whenever you say, "Here I am, just as I am" everything falls away and it is no longer necessary to answer your own questioning mind. That which is perpetual and real in you can now live and express. Remember, you now have come to that part of you that is eternally true. There is no longer any need for judgment, juggling, forcing, or scheming, for now every power on earth and in heaven will rush forth to sustain you. It is only in the light of God that we see ourselves as we truly are.

Stand still, regardless of appearances, for you have never been separated from God and therefore no excuses, no explanation, no alibi, no grovelling, no crawling, no floundering, no appeasement, no promising. For when you have presented yourself just as you are, you have done your part. God will do the rest. You will not say again, "I live" but rather, "God lives me."

This is your final responsibility, for now it is God's responsibility. The things we came to do, the things that are welled up within us, the fulfillment we have sought for years, can now be done, for now we have relinquished ourselves to God.

Love yourself and let the inner enthusiasm of God fill every fiber of your being. It does not matter if you stand knee-deep in failure and inadequacy; all is now in the care and keeping of God and you can go free.

How to free the spiritual power within?

Let us cease our constant striving. We have belonged to this old race of struggling humanity long enough. We must learn to free the power of Spirit within us. We limit ourselves by holding onto our difficulties, by not letting go. We focus our mind on situations and conditions. We need to get away from the old idea that we must oversee everything. If we would let it, everything necessary to our life would be taken care of directly from God within us.

God is the unfolding power in the universe, God—in the midst of us. We are always telling God what to do. We are always giving the orders. We must leave to the All-Wisdom, the God-presence, the task of taking care of us. We have become so efficient that we have shut out the Power that is all-sufficiency at all times. We just don't let the wisdom of God unfold in us, because we know too much. Because of his great intellectual efficiency, man has cut off in himself the source of his inspiration and guidance.

No one can take anything away from you, because the Spirit of God is unfolding in and through you—unless you think they can and let them. No one can give you your good unless you open your mind and heart to it—not even God himself. God must have free-flow through us. He needs a pliable, relaxed, peaceful being in whom to carry on His mighty work. He needs a consciousness that is a conductor of spirit. We have closed spirit out of our life because we live in a state of consciousness incompatible with spirit. Build oneness with God and this oneness will take care of all things.

Look at yourself and realize how wonderful you are. Life is the activity of God, but for you it will be what you make it. "The Spirit of God hath made me, and the breath of the Almighty hath given me life. . . . Is not my help in me?" (Job 33:4; 6:13). The "wrath of God" is the blow that awakens. We live in the cosmos, not chaos. God maintains His own integrity; can we maintain ours? But how long must we go on grinding out the lessons of life without learning the joy of living? "Awake thou that sleepest" (Eph. 5:14).

12. The Beginning, Not the End

Man stands at the end of a dark night in spiritual unfoldment. He is being ushered into light and peace. Mankind has been on a very long journey and, whether man is aware of it or not, the tortuous part of the path is passed.

Man has striven for so long, he has tried so many times, prayed so desperately, seemingly without avail, that he has been at wit's end. He has tried everything the outer world has to offer, only to add to his restlessness and confusion.

Do you think man has failed? Do you think the world is lost? Do you think conditions in the world are irreparable? Do you think that God, who created the heavens and the earth and all living and nonliving things, is not able to take care of his creation? Do we have a God who is all-powerful but cannot keep safe his own?

What kind of God do you think we have? Do you think that man, the executive power, creator of the outer world, is not directed by a greater power?

Do you think that no matter how hard we struggle to find our way, to do what is right, to love when it is difficult to love, it only leads to failure? Do you think that pressing forward when we are unable to see ahead will be to no avail?

Can you understand that a great and glorious preparation is in progress, that it has been going on since the beginning of time?

Each prayer, desire, and reaching out was like a root sent down in the earth. Unseen, all these will finally form the power that will sustain the plant that is to come, as all the thoughts, feelings, and experiences of man will form the unseen power for the fulfilled man.

Remember that every moment of fear, every hurt, tear, and prayer will pay off, and that the times you stood unwavering have built a *well* of consciousness that is now ready to sustain you.

We think of the seed in the ground, the bird in the egg, the butterfly in the cocoon, and realize that they are in the process of preparation; but we forget that we too have been through preparation. To us, this preparation may have seemed a waste of time, a great personal challenge, frustration, sickness, or outer failure—but failure, as we call it, is not what we think it is. Every failure is a part of our being made ready for a particular purpose, for a much greater expression of good.

Do not try to solve the mystery of why things happen to you and to others. Do not ask why that failure or why that success. Success is always built on many failures. Do not ask, "Why does he do that?" or "Why do people react this way?" Do not ask such foolish questions. First, you could not possibly answer such questions and, second, you yourself become involved in wondering and anxiety, which can only delay your awareness of this great time which is at hand.

The time of acceptance and fulfillment lies before us. It is the coming forth of man's permanent good. It is not the beginning of some great problem but the end result of preparation.

All that has been called loss and defeat is only to qualify each of us for further development. This has been going on in the case of mankind for eons and eons, and in the case of individuals for many lifetimes. So much has gone on in the unfolding and fitting of man for this, the present day; man, not understanding, has only known it as fear, trouble, and unhappiness.

In our individual lives, every frustration, disappointment, failure, unanswered prayer, the letting go of precious ideas on which we had placed much store, and the hopes that fizzled out were all preparation. Sometimes our experiences are like leaves that fall from the tree, seemingly of no value; but, falling at the root of the tree, they fertilize the soil to make the fruit to come more valuable and the tree more productive.

Are you ready to know that God has brought all of mankind, including you and me, by devious ways, to this present day, to this precious moment in time, for a *purpose?* We have come for the most high purpose—"We know that all things work together for good to them that love God, to them who are called according to his purpose" (Rom. 8:28). We have arrived at the place where we can become great enough to accept *all*—our complete heritage. *The time has come for us to be our God-self.* "If God be for us, who can be against us?" (Rom. 8:31).

LOOK FORWARD

Don't look back on the way that you have come. Look forward to that which lies ahead. This is the time to deliver your greater self, "for it is the Father's good pleasure to give you the Kingdom" (Luke 12:32). While you are in the process of accepting your own fulfillment, be sure you keep sweet. You may ask, "What is it to keep sweet?" Don't sour on life; don't get bitter. Walk through whatever lies before you, today, with complete awareness that it is not the end but only the beginning.

The night of man's consciousness is passing; physical suffering, destruction, and conflict are waning. Remember the words of the poet William Cowper.

> *Beware of desp'rate steps!*
> *The darkest day*
> *Live till tomorrow will have*
> *Pass'd away.*
> (*The Needless Alarm*)

Life, light, and goodness are at hand. The whole truth is that man cannot escape God; he cannot escape the good. The scales are falling from his eyes. He must see himself as he is and not as he appears to be. The appearances are not destroyed, but the truth is known. We can cheat, lie, and be afraid, but all outer power is a deception. It is ignorance. The whole of our former way of life is being overturned.

It will not be a matter of curing our fears and diseases and making life as comfortable as possible. There will be no compromise between the old way of life and the new. We proclaim the allness of God whenever something threatens our way of life, but during the rest of the time we want to rest comfortably in a world we have always known. This cannot be.

We think health is acquired by following the laws of hygiene. We believe money is earned by our own cleverness. We accept wisdom as acquired by our own intelligence. These are all beliefs in separation from God, but since we call such things good we cling to them. We must know that there is an inner Power in us that does all things, even though it is difficult for us to go past this acceptance at this time.

We cannot see a higher good than just being well, having money, and thinking how clever we are. Even this outer good endangers us, for we let go of the truth of life. War, hate, greed, and all that destroys in the world comes from the belief that we have power. All power moves from the inner citadel of Spirit. All activity, all responsibility, all authority belongs to an unseen Source in us all. It is not human endeavor that implements the power of God; human endeavor objectifies the idea of the power.

Do not decide how the world problems will be settled. Rather, believe in a Power that takes care of all that concerns us. The mind is the battlefield of this age. As at the prophesied Armageddon, we are outnumbered, unarmed against the overlords, but we shall win.

The proud kings of the earth, great men, rich men, mighty men, chiefs, captains, bondmen, and freemen will seek a common safety—a simple faith and belief in a Power that takes care of all. Our greatest good is coming forth—but we are challenged only to heal us forever from all fear.

Crops cannot be gathered without cutting the grain; wine cannot be made without crushing the grapes. They seem to be destroyed but they are really being fulfilled. There is a sharp sickle of knowing, for the harvest of the earth is ripe. We are all being awakened! We stand at the end of many dark experiences, and are about to be ushered into light and awareness.

Let's not look back on the way we have come; let's look forward to what lies ahead! The prophecy says that "every knee shall bow . . . every tongue shall confess . . . then every one of us shall give account of himself to God" (Rom. 14:11, 12).

How could a thing happen that would awaken all mankind? How could a single revelation change every living soul in this mixed-up world?

Through the womb of man's mind, the whole world has come into visibility and audibility. The vast communication system that man has created grows by leaps and bounds. Television and radio are finding their way into the darkest corners of the world and will finally cover the earth. This great power was not created for the hopeless purpose for which it is now used. It was not meant to dull man's mind with stories, advertisements, and reports that stupefy and stultify his indwelling Power. Man has lost contact with the inner Source that sets him free. Instead of using for good the great Essence of Life that solves, resolves, and dissolves all that is untrue, man sits in a lethargic stupor before his television set, morbidly detached from the real things of life. He is indifferent to God and the promptings of his own heart and soul. Man is hypnotized by his own creation, unaware of the Creator, his God-self.

"God himself that formed the earth and made it; he hath established it, he created it not in vain" (Isa. 45:18).

This great network that man has unfolded and that he uses so foolishly was created for a great and special purpose; it may well be the means by which "the deaf [shall] hear . . . and the eyes of the blind shall see out of obscurity, and out of darkness" (Isa. 29:18). Soon it will be possible for every human being on this globe to hear, see, and become aware of some great revelation. We live in a time when there will be great disclosures that will awe and even frighten man. All mankind is ready for a revelation from God; this is what lies before us, not destruction as some would have you think.

Let us agree that every ear could hear and every eye could see; still the human mind asks, "In this world of dissension and opposition, is there a human being that would be capable and worthy of revealing such a message—a message that could awaken every human being to a peace and power great enough for this time? There is no answer to this question in the measure of the human mind, but the poet William Cowper says: "God moves in a mysterious way his wonders to perform."

The question is, Can man believe in a power he cannot understand with the limitations of his human mind? Can he believe the assurance in Matthew (19:26), that "with God all things are possible"? Much earlier, Jeremiah put his faith into these wonderful old words (32:27): "Behold, I am the Lord, the God of all flesh: is there anything too hard for me?"

Man needs to be shaken and reawakened to the activity of a power that he has lain aside in the heyday of modern life. In this day and time, a man appears to be a fool to believe in an invisible Power that can interfere with and set aside the outer laws of life that man has established. Let us be reminded of these words: "Let no man deceive himself. If any man among you seemeth to be wise in this world, let him become a fool, that he may be wise. For the wisdom of this world is foolishness with God." . . . "He that hath ears to hear, let him hear" (I Cor. 3:18; Mark 4:9).

USA Medical
Ben-bb
1 800
947 7900

Spiritual Qi Gong
unfolder

Your Divine Power
By
Paul L. Hannah as
Master Teacha

Spiritual Qi Gong
Culture
Transparent Race
Spiritual Bery

Roms 12:2 — He is transformed by the Newness of her Mind

How to I let my Inner Most take over my Head and Mind